Reach the Highest Standard
in Professional Learning:
Learning Communities

Volumes in the Reach the Highest Standard in Professional Learning Series

Learning Communities

Leadership

Resources

Data

Learning Designs

Implementation

Outcomes

Reach the Highest Standard in Professional Learning: Learning Communities

Editors
Shirley M. Hord
Patricia Roy

Contributors
Ann Lieberman
Lynne Miller
Valerie von Frank

A Joint Publication

CORWIN
A SAGE Company

FOR INFORMATION:

Corwin
A SAGE Company
2455 Teller Road
Thousand Oaks, California 91320
(800) 233-9936
www.corwin.com

SAGE Publications Ltd.
1 Oliver's Yard
55 City Road
London EC1Y 1SP
United Kingdom

SAGE Publications India Pvt. Ltd.
B 1/I 1 Mohan Cooperative Industrial Area
Mathura Road, New Delhi 110 044
India

SAGE Publications Asia-Pacific Pte. Ltd.
3 Church Street
#10-04 Samsung Hub
Singapore 049483

Printed in the United States of America

A catalog record of this book is available from the Library of Congress.

ISBN 978-1-4522-9183-3

This book is printed on acid-free paper.

Acquisitions Editor: Dan Alpert
Associate Editor: Kimberly Greenberg
Editorial Assistant: Cesar Reyes
Production Editor: Cassandra Margaret Seibel
Copy Editor: Kim Husband
Typesetter: C&M Digitals (P) Ltd.
Proofreader: Susan Schon
Indexer: Jean Casalegno
Cover Designer: Gail Buschman

SUSTAINABLE FORESTRY INITIATIVE

Certified Chain of Custody
Promoting Sustainable Forestry
www.sfiprogram.org
SFI-01268

SFI label applies to text stock

13 14 15 16 17 10 9 8 7 6 5 4 3 2 1

Contents

Introduction to the Series

These are the demands on educators and school systems right now, among many others:

- They must fulfill the moral imperative of educating every child for tomorrow's world, regardless of background or status.
- They must be prepared to implement college- and career-ready standards and related assessments.
- They must implement educator evaluations tied to accountability systems.

A critical element in creating school systems that can meet these demands is building the capacity of the system's educators at all levels, from the classroom teacher to the instructional coach to the school principal to the central office administrator, and including those partners who work within and beyond districts. Building educator capacity in this context requires effective professional learning.

Learning Forward's Standards for Professional Learning define the essential elements of and conditions for professional learning that leads to changed educator practices and improved student results. They are grounded in the understanding that the ultimate purpose of professional learning is increasing student success. Educator effectiveness—and this includes all educators working in and with school systems, not just teachers—is linked closely to student learning. Therefore increasing the effectiveness of educators is a key lever to school improvement.

Effective professional learning happens in a culture of continuous improvement, informed by data about student and educator performance and supported by leadership and sufficient resources.

Educators learning daily have access to information about relevant instructional strategies and resources and, just as important, time for collaboration with colleagues, coaches, and school leaders. Education leaders and systems that value effective professional learning provide not only sufficient time and money but also create structures that reinforce monitoring and evaluation of that learning so they understand what is effective and have information to adjust and improve.

WHY STANDARDS?

Given that any system can—and must—develop expertise about professional learning, why are standards important? Among many reasons are these:

First, adherence to standards ensures equity. When learning leaders across schools and systems agree to follow a common set of guidelines, they are committing to equal opportunities for all the learners in those systems. If all learning is in alignment with the Standards for Professional Learning and tied to student and school improvement goals, then all educators have access to the best expertise available to improve their practice and monitor results.

Standards also provide a common language that allows for conversation, collaboration, and implementation planning that crosses state, regional, and national borders. This collaboration can leverage expertise from any corner of the world to change practice and results.

Finally, standards offer guidelines for accountability. While an endorsement of the standards doesn't in itself guarantee quality, they provide a framework within which systems can establish measures to monitor progress, alignment, and results.

FROM STANDARDS TO TRANSFORMATION

So a commitment to standards is a first critical step. Moving into deep understanding and sustained implementation of standards is another matter. Transforming practices, and indeed, whole systems, will require long-term study, planning, and evaluation.

Reach the Highest Standard in Professional Learning is created to be an essential set of tools to help school and system leaders take those steps. As with the Standards for Professional Learning themselves, there will be seven volumes, one for each standard.

While the standards were created to work in synergy, we know that educators approach professional learning from a wide range of experiences, concerns, expertise, and passions. Perhaps a school leader may have started PLCs in his school to address a particular learning challenge, and thus has an abiding interest in how learning communities can foster teacher quality and better results. Maybe a central office administrator started her journey to standards-based professional learning through a study of how data informs changes, and she wants to learn more about the foundations of data use. This series was created to support such educators and to help them continue on their journey of understanding systemwide improvement and the pieces that make such transformation possible.

In developing this series of books on the Standards for Professional Learning, Corwin and Learning Forward envisioned that practitioners would enter this world of information through one particular book, and that their needs and interests would take them to all seven as the books are developed. The intention is to serve the range of needs practitioners bring and to support a full understanding of the elements critical to effective professional learning.

All seven volumes in Reach the Highest Standard in Professional Learning share a common structure, with components to support knowledge development, exploration of changes in practice, and a vision of each concept at work in real-world settings.

In each volume, readers will find

- A think piece developed by a leading voice in the professional learning field. These thought leaders represent both scholars and practitioners, and their work invites readers to consider the foundations of each standard and to push understanding of those seven standards.
- An implementation piece that helps readers put the think piece and related ideas into practice, with tools for both individuals and groups to use in reflection and discussion about the standards. Shirley M. Hord and Patricia Roy, series editors and longstanding Learning Forward standards leaders, created the implementation pieces across the entire series.
- A case study that illuminates what it looks like in schools and districts when education leaders prioritize the standards in

their improvement priorities. Valerie von Frank, with many years of writing about education in general and professional learning in particular, reported these pieces, highlighting insights specific to each standard.

MOVING TOWARD TRANSFORMATION

We know this about effective professional learning: Building awareness isn't enough to change practice. It's a critical first piece, and these volumes will help in knowledge development. But sustaining knowledge and implementing change require more.

Our intention is that the content and structure of the volumes can move readers from awareness to changes in practice to transformation of systems. And of course transformation requires much more. Commitment to a vision for change is an exciting place to start. A long-term informed investment of time, energy, and resources is non-negotiable, as is leadership that transcends one visionary leader who will inevitably move on.

Ultimately, it will be the development of a culture of collective responsibility for all students that sustains improvement. We invite you to begin your journey toward developing that culture through study of the Standards for Professional Learning and through Reach the Highest Standard in Professional Learning. Learning Forward will continue to support the development of knowledge, tools, and evidence that inform practitioners and the field. Next year's challenges may be new ones, and educators working at their full potential will always be at the core of reaching our goals for students.

Stephanie Hirsh
Executive Director, Learning Forward

The Learning Forward Standards for Professional Learning

Learning Communities: Professional learning that increases educator effectiveness and results for all students occurs within learning communities committed to continuous improvement, collective responsibility, and goal alignment.

Leadership: Professional learning that increases educator effectiveness and results for all students requires skillful leaders who develop capacity, advocate, and create support systems for professional learning.

Resources: Professional learning that increases educator effectiveness and results for all students requires prioritizing, monitoring, and coordinating resources for educator learning.

Data: Professional learning that increases educator effectiveness and results for all students uses a variety of sources and types of student, educator, and system data to plan, assess, and evaluate professional learning.

Learning Designs: Professional learning that increases educator effectiveness and results for all students integrates theories, research, and models of human learning to achieve its intended outcomes.

Implementation: Professional learning that increases educator effectiveness and results for all students applies research on change and sustains support for implementation of professional learning for long-term change.

Outcomes: Professional learning that increases educator effectiveness and results for all students aligns its outcomes with educator performance and student curriculum standards.

Source: Learning Forward. (2011). *Standards for Professional Learning.* Oxford, OH: Author.

The Learning Communities Standard

Professional learning that increases educator effectiveness and results for all students occurs within learning communities committed to continuous improvement, collective responsibility, and goal alignment.

Professional learning within communities requires continuous improvement, promotes collective responsibility, and supports alignment of individual, team, school, and school system goals. Learning communities convene regularly and frequently during the workday to engage in collaborative professional learning to strengthen their practice and increase student results. Learning community members are accountable to one another to achieve the shared goals of the school and school system and work in transparent, authentic settings that support their improvement.

ENGAGE IN CONTINUOUS IMPROVEMENT

Learning communities apply a cycle of continuous improvement to engage in inquiry, action research, data analysis, planning, implementation, reflection, and evaluation. Characteristics of each application of the cycle of continuous improvement are:

- The use of data to determine student and educator learning needs;
- Identification of shared goals for student and educator learning;

- Professional learning to extend educators' knowledge of content, content-specific pedagogy, how students learn, and management of classroom environments;
- Selection and implementation of appropriate evidence-based strategies to achieve student and educator learning goals;
- Application of the learning with local support at the work site;
- Use of evidence to monitor and refine implementation; and
- Evaluation of results.

DEVELOP COLLECTIVE RESPONSIBILITY

Learning communities share collective responsibility for the learning of all students within the school or school system. Collective responsibility brings together the entire education community, including members of the education workforce—teachers, support staff, school system staff, and administrators—as well as families, policymakers, and other stakeholders, to increase effective teaching in every classroom. Within learning communities, peer accountability rather than formal or administrative accountability ignites commitment to professional learning. Every student benefits from the strengths and expertise of every educator when communities of educators learn together and are supported by local communities whose members value education for all students.

Collective participation advances the goals of a whole school or team as well as those of individuals. Communities of caring, analytic, reflective, and inquiring educators collaborate to learn what is necessary to increase student learning. Within learning communities, members exchange feedback about their practice with one another, visit each other's classrooms or work settings, and share resources. Learning community members strive to refine their collaboration, communication, and relationship skills to work within and across both internal and external systems to support student learning. They develop norms of collaboration and relational trust and employ processes and structures that unleash expertise and strengthen capacity to analyze, plan, implement, support, and evaluate their practice.

While some professional learning occurs individually, particularly to address individual development goals, the more one educator's learning is shared and supported by others, the more quickly the culture of continuous improvement, collective responsibility, and high expectations for students and educators grows. Collective responsibility and participation foster peer-to-peer support for learning and maintain a consistent focus on shared goals within and across communities. Technology facilitates and expands community interaction, learning, resource archiving and sharing, and knowledge construction and sharing. Some educators may meet with peers virtually in local or global communities to focus on individual, team, school, or school system improvement goals. Often supported through technology, cross-community communication within schools, across schools, and among school systems reinforces shared goals, promotes knowledge construction and sharing, strengthens coherence, taps educators' expertise, and increases access to and use of resources.

Communities of learners may be various sizes, include members with similar or different roles or responsibilities, and meet frequently face-to-face, virtually, or through a combination. Educators may be members of multiple learning communities. Some communities may include members who share common students, areas of responsibility, roles, interests, or goals. Learning communities tap internal and external expertise and resources to strengthen practice and student learning. Because the education system reaches out to include students, their families, community members, the education workforce, and public officials who share responsibility for student achievement, some learning communities may include representatives of these groups.

CREATE ALIGNMENT AND ACCOUNTABILITY

Professional learning that occurs within learning communities provides an ongoing system of support for continuous improvement and implementation of school and systemwide initiatives. To avoid fragmentation among learning communities and to strengthen their contribution to school and system goals, public officials and school system leaders create policies that establish formal accountability for results along with the support needed to achieve results. To be effective, these policies and supports align with an explicit vision and goals for successful learning communities. Learning communities align their goals with those of the school and school system, engage in continuous professional learning, and hold all members collectively accountable for results.

The professional learning that occurs within learning communities both supports and is supported by policy and governance, curriculum and instruction, human resources, and other functions within a school system. Learning communities bridge the knowing-doing gap by transforming macro-level learning—knowledge and skill development—into micro-level learning—the practices and refinements necessary for full implementation in the classroom or workplace. When professional learning occurs within a system driven by high expectations, shared goals, professionalism, and peer accountability, the outcome is deep change for individuals and systems.

RELATED RESEARCH

Bolam, R., McMahon, A., Stoll, L., Thomas, S., & Wallace, M. (with Greenwood, A., et al.). (2005, May). *Creating and sustaining effective professional learning communities* (Research Brief RB637). Nottingham, United Kingdom: Department for Education and Skills.

Hord, S. M. (Ed.). (2004). *Learning together, leading together: Changing schools through professional learning communities.* New York: Teachers College Press & NSDC.

Lieberman, A., & Miller, L. (Eds.) (2008). *Teachers in professional communities: Improving teaching and learning.* New York: Teachers College Press.

McLaughlin, M. W., & Talbert, J. E. (2001). *Professional communities and the work of high school teaching.* Chicago: University of Chicago Press.

Saunders, W. M., Goldenberg, C. N., & Gallimore, R. (2009, December). Increasing achievement by focusing grade-level teams on improving classroom learning: A prospective, quasi-experimental study of Title I schools. *American Educational Research Journal, 46*(4), 1006–1033.

Source: Learning Forward. (2011). *Standards for Professional Learning.* Oxford, OH: Author.

About the Series Editors

Dr. Shirley M. Hord, PhD, is the scholar laureate of Learning Forward (previously National Staff Development Council), following her retirement as Scholar Emerita at the Southwest Educational Development Laboratory in Austin, Texas. There she directed the Strategies for Increasing Student Success Program. She continues to design and coordinate professional development activities related to educational change and improvement, school leadership, and the creation of professional learning communities.

Her early roles as elementary school classroom teacher and university science education faculty at The University of Texas at Austin were followed by her appointment as co-director of Research on the Improvement Process at the Research and Development Center for Teacher Education at The University of Texas at Austin. There she administered and conducted research on school improvement and the role of school leaders in school change.

She served as a fellow of the National Center for Effective Schools Research and Development and was U.S. representative to the Foundation for the International School Improvement Project, an international effort that develops research, training, and policy initiatives to support local school improvement practices.

In addition to working with educators at all levels across the U.S. and Canada, Hord makes presentations and consults in Asia, Europe, Australia, Africa, and Mexico.

Her current interests focus on the creation and functioning of educational organizations as learning communities and the role of leaders who serve such organizations. Dr. Hord is the author of numerous articles and books, of which a selection of the most recent are *Implementing Change: Patterns, Principles, and Potholes,* 3rd ed. (with Gene E. Hall, 2011); *Reclaiming Our Teaching Profession: The Power of Educators Learning in Community* (with Edward F. Tobia, 2012); and *A Playbook for Professional Learning: Putting the Standards Into Action* (with Stephanie Hirsh, 2012).

 **Dr. Patricia Roy** is a senior consultant with Learning Forward's Center for Results. She works with state departments of education, districts, and schools across the United States as well as internationally. Most recently, she developed briefings and a resource guide to help schools use results from the revised Standards Assessment Inventory (SAI2) to improve professional learning. She has authored many articles and chapters on effective professional development, school improvement, innovation configuration maps, and cooperative learning. In her work with Learning Forward, Pat developed professional learning resource toolkits for Georgia; Arkansas; and Rochester, NY. She co-authored with Joellen Killion, *Becoming a Learning School* and with Stephanie Hirsh, Joellen Killion, and Shirley Hord, *Standards Into Practice: Innovation Configurations for School-Based Roles* (2012). For five years, she wrote columns about implementing the Standards for Professional Development for *The Learning Principal* and *The Learning System,* two Learning Forward newsletters. She has also served as faculty for Professional Development Leadership Academy through the Arizona Department of Education. This 3-year program developed the knowledge and skills of school and district teams to plan, implement, and evaluate professional learning. She has also served as the founding director of the Delaware Professional Development Center in Dover, DE. The Center, developed by the Delaware State Education Association, focused on school improvement for student achievement and effective professional learning. She also served as the director of the Center for School Change in connection with a National Science Foundation SSI grant, a district coordinator of staff development, and an administrator in a regional educational consortium in Minnesota. Creating and improving professional learning so that it impacts student achievement is one of Pat's passions.

About the Contributors

Dr. Ann Lieberman currently serves as senior scholar and interim executive director of the Stanford Center for Opportunity Policy in Education at Stanford University. Ann was previously a senior scholar at the Carnegie Foundation for the Advancement of Teaching and is professor emeritus of education at Teachers College, Columbia University. Lieberman is widely known for her work in the areas of teacher leadership and development, collaborative research, networks and school-university partnerships, and the problems and prospects for understanding educational change.

Her latest book is *Mentoring Teachers: Navigating the Real World Tensions* (with S. Hanson and J. Gless). Her other books include *Inside the National Writing Project: Connecting Network Learning and Classroom Teaching* (with Diane Wood), *Teachers: Transforming Their World and Their Work*, and *Teachers in Professional Learning Communities: Improving Teaching and Learning* (with Lynne Miller). Lieberman has served on numerous national and international advisory boards, including those of the United Federation of Teachers and the National Education Association. She is also a past president of the American Educational Research Association. As a researcher she is currently working on deepening the field's understanding of different structures that support school reform including networks, partnerships, and coalitions. She has recently been to Shanghai and Finland as a speaker and a learner. She was a keynote speaker in Beijing at the end of April speaking at a conference on "Teacher as Researcher." Lieberman received her BA and EdD at UCLA and her MA at California State University at Northridge, where she also received an honorary degree.

Dr. Lynne Miller, EdD, is professor of educational leadership and executive director of the Southern Maine Partnership at the University of Southern Maine. Before joining the USM faculty in 1987, she held a variety of positions in public schools and universities, including secondary English teacher and director of a public alternative high school in Philadelphia; assistant professor/Teacher Corps instructor at the University of Massachusetts; desegregation consultant in Boston; and assistant principal and associate superintendent in South Bend, Indiana.

Lynne continues to attempt to do what Ted Sizer calls "walking the fault line between theory and practice" as an engaged scholar and activist. She has written widely in the field of teacher development and school reform. In addition to authoring numerous articles, chapters, and papers, she has completed six books with Ann Lieberman, the most recent of which are *Teachers Caught in the Action* (Teachers College Press, 2001) and *Teacher Leadership* (Jossey-Bass, 2004). Lynne is an active participant in local and national reform efforts. She was an original member of the National Commission on Teaching and America's Future and now serves on the policy advisory board of the Promising School Project in Maine, sponsored by the Bill and Melinda Gates Foundation. She is currently engaged in connecting high school and college faculty in efforts to prepare more students for success in higher education.

Valerie von Frank is an author, editor, and communications consultant. A former newspaper editor and education reporter, she has focused much of her writing on education issues, including professional learning. She served as communications director in an urban school district and a nonprofit school reform organization and was the editor of *JSD*, the flagship magazine for the National Staff Development Council, now Learning Forward, for seven years. She has written extensively for publications, including *JSD, Tools for Schools, The Learning System, The Learning Principal,* and *T3.* She is coauthor with Ann Delehant of *Making Meetings Work: How to Get Started, Get Going, and Get It Done* (Corwin, 2007), with Linda Munger of *Change, Lead, Succeed* (NSDC, 2010), with Robert Garmston of *Unlocking Group Potential to Improve Schools* (Corwin, 2012), and with Jennifer Abrams of *The Multigenerational Workplace: Communicate, Collaborate, and Create Community* (Corwin, 2014).

CHAPTER ONE

Unpacking Professional Learning Communities

Getting From Here to There

Ann Lieberman and Lynne Miller

In 2008, we characterized professional learning communities (PLCs) as "ongoing groups of teachers who meet regularly for the purpose of increasing their own learning and that of their students" (Lieberman & Miller, 2008, p. 2). We have come to think that they are more than that. They are not just a way for teachers to collaborate, nor are they just one more promising approach to staff development. Professional learning communities have gained traction across the globe because of their potential for energizing a larger agenda: to reform schools, improve and professionalize teaching, advance learning for *all* students, and change the discourse about teacher accountability. Why have these communities gained such attention and support now? What do we know about them? In the first two sections of this chapter, we provide a response to these questions. In the third section and fourth sections, we describe three contexts in which professional learning communities have been enacted and consider the challenges professional learning communities face. We conclude with an examination of the questions professional communities raise and the implications they pose for school reform in general and the role of teachers in the reform agenda in particular.

PROFESSIONAL LEARNING COMMUNITIES: WHY NOW?

Policymakers, across the political spectrum, agree that in a globalized world, schools have to ensure high-quality education for all students and to narrow the achievement gap between minority and majority students and between the well off and the poor. What has been and continues to be under contention is how to get from here to there. McGuinn (2010) identified two competing narratives that underlie education policy initiatives: the equity narrative that views poverty as the barrier to reform and the accountability narrative that views inadequate standards for students and teachers as the problem.

Rooted in the civil rights movement and antipoverty initiatives of the 1960s, the equity narrative gained credence in Title One of the Elementary and Secondary School Act of 1965, which provided direct funding to schools with poor and underachieving students. The Coleman Report of 1966, which concluded that student disparities in achievement were due to conditions of poverty and that schools made little difference, further legitimized this view. Later iterations of the equity narrative included policies regarding gender, disabilities, and limited English proficiency.

The accountability narrative, on the other hand, places its emphasis on changing schools and teaching rather than on alleviating poverty and focuses on measurable outcomes for both students and teachers as remedies. This narrative was memorably articulated in *A Nation at Risk* (National Commission on Excellence in Education, 1983), whose opening statement was a call to arms.

> If an unfriendly foreign power had attempted to impose on America the mediocre educational performance that exists today, we might well have viewed it as an act of war. . . . We have, in effect, been committing an act of unthinking, unilateral educational disarmament. (p. 8)

The clear message was that if the United States were to remain a world power, it had to hold teachers and schools accountable to higher standards. The report's recommendations looked to the input/output accountability measures of business as the model. The current iteration of this narrative is evident in the No Child Left Behind Act of 2000 and the recent revisions proposed under the Department of Education waiver process, whose provisions call for increased standardized testing, a standards-based curriculum and assessment system, and a teacher evaluation system tied to student test scores. In addition, there are emerging demands on the local level for changes in tenure, hiring, and firing procedures, for closing and reconstituting schools, for establishing charter schools, and for offering alternative teacher recruitment and training pathways.

While the two narratives differ in how they identify the root causes of unequal student outcomes and how they conceive of necessary remedies, they share something in common: They both view teachers and schools as the *objects* of reform and not as actively engaged *subjects*. They deny practitioners a sense of agency, and they fail to provide roles for teachers as full participants in the school reform agenda as problem posers and problem solvers. We need a third narrative, one that acknowledges the external effects of poverty on achievement as well as the internal effects of schools and teachers. We need a narrative that honors teacher knowledge and craft as key ingredients in equalizing outcomes. We think the groundswell of support for professional learning communities supports such a narrative.

What we are recommending is not new. There is a long but muted tradition of teacher-centered and teacher-led school reform that has resonated with teachers in different eras and contexts by giving them a voice in policy and a way to counterbalance initiatives that were designed to exclude them. For example, in the aftermath of the Coleman Report, which rendered teachers almost irrelevant, educators found refuge in teacher centers that provided them with a safe place to meet, share ideas, and collaborate on efforts to improve their practices. Supported by a federal grant program in 1978, the movement gained national momentum; although funds were cut 4 years later, some centers were kept alive through local and state initiatives. Again in the 1980s, in the wake of recommendations of *A Nation at Risk* to apply business metrics to education, teachers and schools embraced the idea of teacher leadership. New positions were created for practicing teachers, giving them the time and the resources to lead in school reform efforts around curriculum and staff development, school restructuring, and assessment and accountability policies and procedures.

Now that we find ourselves in an era of externally driven accountability mandates and in which teachers are pushed to the sidelines of reform, is it any wonder that professional learning communities have captured the imagination of practicing educators and taken hold? Now, as in the past, teachers recognize that they have the knowledge, skill, and power to provide an alternative to top-down mandates and restrictive notions of teaching and learning and to change practice from the bottom up and from the inside out. What better time than now to rekindle the flame of teacher-centered and teacher-led school reform?

WHAT WE KNOW ABOUT PROFESSIONAL LEARNING COMMUNITIES

Professional learning communities in education owe much to the work of two organizational theorists, whose initial inquiries focused on groups outside of education and whose ideas have since been applied to teachers and schools. Don Schon (1983) looked at how architects collaborated on design projects and came up with the idea of *reflective practice,* in which

> The practitioner allows himself to experience surprise, puzzlement, or confusion in a situation which he finds uncertain or unique. He reflects on the phenomenon before him, and on the prior understandings which have been implicit in his behaviour. He carries out an experiment which serves to generate both a new understanding of the phenomenon and a change in the situation. (p. 68)

Schon viewed reflective practice as a precondition for continuous learning. He described two kinds of reflective practice: *reflection in action* and *reflection on action.* It is reflection on action, which entails opportunities for sharing ideas, looking at practice with a critical eye, and jointly identifying problems of practice and hypothesizing about solutions, that is central to professional learning communities in education.

The other thinker is Etienne Wenger, who studied apprentices in the process of becoming full members of a craft guild. He introduced the idea of *communities of practice* in which practitioners develop a shared repertoire of resources that allow them to identify and solve shared problems of practice. Wenger (1998) noted that these communities develop over time and have a powerful presence in the lives of members. They include rituals and routines that affirm membership, engage members in a variety of interactions, provide short- and long-term value, and promote a communal identity and a sense of belonging (Wenger, 1998). Wenger adds to Schon's idea of reflective communities; both contribute to our understanding of the roots of PLCs as communities of practice that engage in reflection on practice. Nonhierarchical and self-governing, they offer opportunities for teachers to reflect on action, to learn from each other, to share resources and insights, to solve problems of practice, and to assume responsibility for results.

In their review of the literature on professional learning communities, Vesco, Ross, and Adams (2008) investigated the effects of professional learning communities on three outcomes: teacher practice, school culture, and student achievement. In terms of teacher practice, they found evidence that teachers who participated in professional learning communities viewed their practice as having changed in the direction of student centeredness, though there were few descriptions of the specific pedagogical practices that had changed. When it came to effects on school culture, the researchers found substantial evidence that PLCs led to increased teacher collaboration, more focus on student learning, expanded teacher authority over instructional decisions, and the establishment of norms of continuous learning. In terms of effects on student achievement, the researchers concluded that the few controlled studies that were done indicated improvement in student test scores in schools where teacher collaboration was complemented by "structured work that was highly focused around student learning" (Vesco et al., 2008, p. 15). They found no evidence of effects on student achievement where this structured work was absent. At issue with this and all effectiveness studies is that the goals under study tend to be limited to quantifiable variables and that student achievement is narrowly defined as growth on standardized measures.

There is a growing body of research that provides a wider lens for viewing professional learning communities and that broadens the idea of "effectiveness" as a focus of inquiry. Qualitative in nature, these studies document the development and growth of professional learning communities and how they enact conditions that enable them to develop and grow. Talbert (2010, p. 257) identified four such conditions:

- Norms of collaboration
- Focus on students and their academic performance
- Access to a wide range of learning resources for individuals and the group
- Mutual accountability for student growth and success

These conditions draw attention to the multiple dimensions of the "structured work" in which members of professional learning communities engage.

Cochran-Smith and Lytle (1993) described how successive professional learning communities that met in a university setting structured their work around inquiry into practice. The groups met for 12 months and included student teachers, faculty, and supervisors from the university and cooperating teachers from different schools in the area. Group members engaged in ongoing collaborative inquiry into a wide variety of issues, including "language and literacy, curriculum and pedagogy; race, class, gender; modes of assessment; and the cultures of schools and teaching" (Cochran-Smith & Lytle, 1993, p. 66) and how they impacted learning and teaching. In their later writings, Cochran-Smith and Lytle (2009) reported how community members documented and made public the changes they made in their instructional practices and how these impacted observed student learning and engagement.

Little and Horn (2007) and Horn (2005) reported on a learning community that developed in one high school and consisted of nine math teachers who met every week to work on ways to improve their teaching of algebra, to increase student math achievement, and to add to enrollments in advanced classes. The group members used a structured "check-in" to jump-start each session. During this time, each participant was invited to present a problem of practice or a new idea for group consideration. The honest and direct talk that followed focused on both teaching practice and student learning; it was a way for the members to develop norms of collaboration and to hold each other accountable to the group for their practice. This dual emphasis on teacher and student learning had its desired results; the researchers reported changes in teaching practices and teacher leadership roles as well as an increase in student engagement and in the number of students taking higher-level math courses.

McLaughlin and Talbert's (2001) ambitious study of 22 schools in Michigan and California provides insight into teaching communities within schools. The researchers identified three kinds of teaching communities and reported on the degree to which their differing teaching cultures, professional norms and values, and instructional practices influenced innovation, promoted reform, and affected student engagement and academic outcomes. *Weak communities* were characterized by teacher isolation, a high priority on teacher seniority in course assignment, text-based teaching practices based on a transmission model, and low expectations for students. In these communities, students were minimally engaged and showed little change in attainment levels. *Strong-traditional communities,* where teacher isolation was less pronounced and collegiality more normative, were characterized by sorting students by academic ability, differentiated student expectations (high for the most able, lower for others), seniority-based course assignments, and grading on a curve. In these schools, the highly tracked students demonstrated a high level of engagement and attainment, and the lower-tracked students did not fare so well. McLaughlin and Talbert (2001) viewed these communities as being "stuck" in terms of innovation and reform.

In what they termed *strong teacher communities,* McLaughlin and Talbert (2001) identified characteristics that set these groups apart from the strong-traditional communities. These included (1) teacher collaboration around problems of teaching and learning, (2) a belief that all students could learn, (3) high expectations for all students, (4) nontracked classrooms, (5) a focus on developing a shared language and knowledge about teaching and learning, and (6) a commitment to active engagement and equitable achievement for all students. McLaughlin and Talbert (2006) considered these strong teacher communities to be "moving" toward innovation and reform and noted the essential role of principal support in their success. In these schools, there was evidence of increased student engagement and gains in achievement.

McLaughlin and Talbert (2006) dug deeper into the strong teacher communities and described their stages of development. The first stage is the *novice stage* in which teachers begin to focus on shared inquiry and do so by collecting data.

The second stage is the *intermediate stage*; here teachers move beyond the mere collection of data and begin to examine the data collectively, to develop a shared language and goals for their work, and to build leadership skills. The third stage is the *advanced stage.* Here the teachers consider how to change their practices in order to improve student outcomes, take on the reform agenda and make it their own, and accept shared responsibility for student learning.

Grossman, Wineburg, and Woolworth (2001) also described the stages in the development of a professional learning community. Working in one high school, they organized and documented the progress of a community of teachers of English and social studies who were charged with creating an interdisciplinary course. They identified three stages of development. The first stage was the *beginning stage* in which teachers were involved in the formation of group identity and playacted at being a community, forming what was in effect a *pseudo-community.* The second stage was the *evolution stage;* here teachers engaged in a process of *navigating the fault lines.* They competed for attention, negotiated their tensions, and fought through their differences. The final stage was the *maturity stage.* When the group reached this stage, they took responsibility for each other and assumed "communal responsibility for individual growth" (Grossman, Wineburg, & Woolworth, 2001). Like the McLaughlin and Talbert (2006) study, this study demonstrates a movement from individual to communal work and demonstrates the dynamics of growth and change of a community over time.

The research discussed here adds to our understanding of professional learning communities across a variety of venues. They highlight how work gets structured and focused on both student achievement and teacher learning, how norms of collaboration are built, how learning resources are used, and how by making their work public to colleagues, teachers assume collective responsibility for their own learning and that of their students—and, in so doing, expand the idea of what it means to be an effective professional learning community.

PROFESSIONAL LEARNING COMMUNITIES IN PRACTICE

Professional learning communities take many forms, and they develop in diverse contexts. A growing number like the algebra study group and the humanities group are *sui generis,* emerging from and staying within the confines of one school. Others, like regional math circles, writing collectives, teacher research groups, and early childhood study groups, are developed on a wider scale and include teachers within a specific geographical area who share common interests and concerns. More recently, electronic communities have begun growing up and engaging teachers nationally and internationally in conversations and shared work through online and blended formats and social media.

We take the position that understanding the dynamics of professional learning communities requires a close-up lens on the tensions and nuances that surface throughout the process of forming and sustaining such communities.

In this section, we focus on two communities that we know well and describe them from the inside out, focusing on how they got started and how they think about and organize their work.

The National Writing Project (NWP) was started by a secondary English teacher who felt strongly that teachers can learn best by being taught by other teachers; and the Southern Maine Partnership was started during a time when school–university partnerships appeared to be the best way to connect the learning of the field, with the knowledge of the university in partnership. For this chapter, we chose to focus on the National Writing Project and the Southern Maine Partnership, as each of them had been around for a long time and we could document how the communities got started, the nature of their collaboration, and the array of practices and policies that became the hallmark of their successes.

The *National Writing Project (NWP)* is the longest-lasting professional learning network in the United States. Initiated in 1974 by high school English teacher Jim Gray, the NWP has grown exponentially and has involved hundreds of teachers in professional learning communities in more than 200 sites. Gray saw that many of his colleagues were using instructional strategies that they learned over time and that were far better than those presented by the external experts who came to his school. He came up with the simple yet compelling idea that teachers should teach teachers.

The Los Angeles site of the NWP, like other network sites, develops its community during a 5-week summer institute. During the institute, teachers engage in the practice of writing; they offer and receive feedback about their writing; they teach their best lesson to peers; they read and critique research relevant to their practice; and they share the literature that they use in their classrooms. The unifying idea is that teachers don't come as empty slates; they possess a great deal of knowledge about teaching and learning that can be harnessed and shared. The institute, then, begins with what teachers know. This one idea empowers participants to recognize the value of teacher knowledge—theirs and that of other community members. They become energized by the open and honest communication that follows: They open up to working with complete strangers and making them colleagues who have lived common experiences. They learn to share, to give feedback, and to accept helpful critique.

Lieberman and Wood (2002) uncovered 11 social practices that are enacted in the NWP site. They included: (1) approaching each colleague as a valuable contributor, (2) honoring teacher knowledge, (3) creating public forums for sharing, (4) the presence of dialogue and critique, (5) turning ownership over to learners, (6) situating learning in practice and relationships, (7) providing multiple entry points into the community, (8) guiding reflection on teaching and learning, (9) sharing leadership, (10) promoting an "inquiry stance," and (11) encouraging a reconceptualization of professional identity linked to membership in the community. Teachers internalize these practices through the common experiences of presenting a favorite lesson, getting feedback on their writing, and reading and discussing literature and research. The "author's chair," a tradition in the NWP, is a defining element of the institute. A teacher reads a piece of her writing while seated in the chair. When she is done reading, she receives feedback from other members and then uses these comments to revise her work. The author's chair is the link between teacher and student learning; teachers employ this strategy in their classrooms as a way to enhance student writing. But the nature of working together, getting and giving feedback, and learning from one another is also learned and used in their classrooms back home.

The NWP is unique in that the summer institute gives rise to local professional communities, and the Los Angeles site spawned many communities throughout the region. Tied together by the core beliefs and practices that are the guts of the summer institute, these communities take shape and provide opportunities for members to continue to learn from each other, to solve the problems of practice, to develop critiques of current policies, and to assume leadership in efforts to improve teaching and learning.

The second professional community we highlight also developed within a broader network, the *Southern Maine Partnership,* a regional school–university collaboration that has been in existence since 1985. Part of the work of the Partnership is to engage school and university educators in critical conversation about their practice and to encourage changes that would be mutually beneficial. A group of superintendents took this idea to a new level in 1997. Critiquing the university's leadership program as a series of disconnected courses attached to an internship, they proposed a new and collaborative approach that became known as Leadership for Tomorrow's Schools (LTS). Now in its ninth iteration, LTS functions as a professional learning community that exists within a master's degree program and brings together 26 teachers from six Partnership districts in shared inquiry, learning, and leadership work for 2 of the 3 years of the degree program.

The group meets weekly to engage in discussion of common readings, to review current research, and to share insights and practices. The conversation continues through blogs in which members post further reflections and come up with new avenues to explore. There are two defining elements of the LTS community: the presentation of "records of practice" and collaboration on ways to bring their insights and understandings to their home school communities.

The idea for "records of practice" developed from a growing concern among members about the lack of a shared knowledge base and common vocabulary about teaching and learning and the absence of an accessible and consistent way to share and reflect on their own practice and to view and comment on that of others. They solved the first problem by deciding that each record should be based in research about effective teaching; they solved the second problem by developing a template for presentation and using conversations during meetings and on the blogs to look at, comment on, and learn from each other's work. The template has six components: an introduction, a brief summary of the research that supports a particular practice, a description of the classroom and its students in which the teacher tried out the practice, a detailed description of what happened, samples of student work, and an evaluation of the process. The records have more than fulfilled their promise and serve as vehicles for collegial support and encouragement and for authentic collaboration and honest talk, as well as for making practice public through online publication and face-to-face presentations.

The second defining element of the LTS community is its commitment to making a contribution that reaches beyond its members. Teachers from each of the six districts meet together as a group and, in consultation with their administrative leaders, design and implement strategies to bring what they have learned from LTS to their school communities. This might include organizing small-group discussion and reading groups, guiding explorations of recent research, assuming roles as coaches and critical friends to new teachers and peers, creating electronic ways for communicating and sharing practice, speaking with parents and community groups, making presentations to school boards and policymakers, developing new curricula and instructional programs, and introducing the idea of records of practice. In reporting on earlier LTS communities,

Lieberman and Miller (2004) viewed making a contribution beyond the community as evidence of a core commitment to leadership development, that in "performing the practice leadership" (p. 49) in small groups, participants were learning not only how to deepen their own practice but also how to influence the practice of others.

Challenges

Change is always difficult, no matter how small or grandiose. Whether it is a new textbook or the introduction of an entirely new curriculum, a revised report card or a complete revision of assessments, the push to do something different raises anxiety and resistance because it requires giving up what is known and embracing what is new. In most cases what is being lost is a familiar practice or favorite approach. In the bureaucratic culture of schools, these changes are usually externally driven, managed from above, and tightly monitored and evaluated.

In professional learning communities, change is more complex and confounding. For teachers, it means having to learn how to live in and navigate two cultures simultaneously, each with its own norms, values, and ways of doing business. The bureaucratic culture of schools expects and rewards compliance; the professional culture of the learning community promotes and honors experimentation and initiative. The bureaucratic culture of schools rests on a hierarchy of authority and differentiated roles and responsibilities; the professional culture of communities is rooted in egalitarian principles and shared responsibility. The bureaucratic culture of schools is based on norms of privacy and autonomy; PLCs are based on norms of collaboration and collective action. The bureaucratic culture of schools holds individual teachers accountable for student outcomes; the professional culture of PLCs assumes shared responsibility for the teaching practices of its members and their impact on students. As Talbert (2010) reminded us, learning to live in these two cultures is not easy. It challenges teachers to learn to negotiate both worlds, to use dual currencies—that of a long-enduring school culture and that of a newly developing professional culture that requires new ways of thinking and working. In meeting these demands, teachers in professional learning communities face several challenges, among them establishing time and structures for their learning, staying true to purpose and vision, and balancing comprehensive notions of teacher and student learning. Each is discussed in the following paragraphs.

Time presents a major challenge to PLCs; so does structure. Teachers who are often overwhelmed by the dailiness of teaching, the plethora of meetings they are expected to attend, and the detailed reports they have to complete now have to find time for collaborative professional learning as well. While some schools schedule time for learning communities within the school day, they may impose their own agendas and procedures on the groups, with the result that teachers relinquish authorship and control. The challenge, then, is for professional learning communities to find or invent time to meet, to establish and routinize structures, and to keep the focus on both teacher and student learning.

The challenge of staying true to purpose and vision is always present. This means teachers must learn how to collaborate, engage in honest talk, be open with their failures as well as their successes, provide support and encouragement, and relinquish norms of privacy and isolation for norms of disclosure and connection. Learning to collaborate and to "make teaching public" are perhaps the most difficult challenges teachers face in learning communities. As a result of their training and early socialization, teachers have learned to depend primarily on their own experience and private interpretations. Because they grow up in schools that Lortie (1975) characterized as "cellular" organizations that promoted individualism, conservatism, and presentism and in which there is little opportunity to collaborate, teachers hold tightly to their private ideas about what is important and shy away from opening their practice to other sets of eyes. The challenge to professional learning communities is to provide a new set of experiences and new forms of socialization for its members. Collaboration and going public with teaching do not come naturally. They must be organized, nurtured, focused, and supported. And there are no recipes for how to do this.

In addition, communities have to meet the challenge of maintaining a focus on both teacher learning and student learning without subscribing to limited definitions of either. Teacher learning does not mean mastering "evidence-based" and technical teaching practices; it involves more than that. It begins with a willingness to be uncomfortable with taken-for-granted notions of teaching and learning. It entails critical reflection on practice, an openness to change, a disposition to experiment and take risks, a readiness to make an honest assessment of what works, and a desire to want to know why. Student learning is not limited to the mastery of routine skills and easily measured outcomes. It involves being able to transfer knowledge and skills to new and unfamiliar situations, gaining a broad understanding of ideas and phenomena and how to think about them, creating original products and inventions, taking on cognitive challenges, being fully engaged in a task or project, and wanting to know more. This kind of thinking is contrary to what is promoted in the present era of narrow accountability, but it is what holds a PLC together. Data mining does not lead to enhanced student learning; good teaching practice does.

The challenge of influencing practice beyond the community is one that is often overlooked. In focusing on maintaining a community, members run the risk of alienating colleagues and keeping powerful experiences and insights limited to a small and exclusive group. The kind of participation and sharing that teachers learn in PLCs can influence a whole school culture over time; and this requires teacher leadership, as both the NWP and LTS cases demonstrate. Teachers who participate in the Los Angeles site of the NWP are expected to go back to their schools and organize professional learning for their peers. Similarly, members of LTS are expected to share what they have learned with colleagues in their home schools and districts. Principals can also lend support by facilitating resources and providing time and supportive conditions for teacher-led and teacher-driven professional learning. They are in a position to use state policies and garner available resources to help fashion authentic communities. Extending beyond the community will come with its own tensions and challenges around differences in the subject matter demands, varying levels of commitment, and conflicting views about teaching and learning and the purpose of education.

Implications

The challenges that professional learning communities face are not separate; the solutions that develop are interlocked as each community creates its own unique culture. When teachers dedicate time to meet with each other, they can begin to build and routinize the structures necessary to support a professional teaching culture. Collaboration grows over time when there is an agreed-upon focus for the work and a safe place to talk honestly about problems of practice. "Going public" with one's work becomes less threatening in a collaborative culture in which norms of openness and trust are enacted. Staying true to purpose and vision and resisting external efforts to shape agendas around narrow definitions of teacher and student learning gain strength when people have a vested interest in the community, its goals, and its practices. Extending authentic teacher learning beyond the boundary of the community through teacher leadership and principal support builds capacity for a transformation of schooling that policymakers strive for but rarely achieve.

If there are any implications for the future of professional learning communities, they are best derived from lessons learned from practice:

- Develop and nurture a professional teaching culture that provides an alternative to the norms and values of the bureaucratic culture of schools
- Learn how to navigate between the two cultures and leverage bureaucratic mandates for authentic teacher learning
- Dedicate time and resources to the work
- Routinize structures for inquiry, reflection, and collaboration
- Provide vehicles and supports for making teaching public
- Maintain control of the agenda in the face of pressures to do otherwise
- Embrace expansive definitions of teacher development and student learning
- Practice patience and take time to navigate the fault lines that emerge
- Take on issues of equity and accountability and make them your own
- Make an effort to be inclusive rather than exclusive and to share practices and insights with a larger community of educators

Creating professional learning communities is one of the most important reform ideas we have had in a long time. As this chapter shows, it may also be one of the most difficult and challenging, not because it is inherently complicated but because it goes against the norms that most schools have inadvertently created—teachers living in isolation. And teachers must unlearn many of the practices that have become ingrained in the structure of schools and build communities of practice shared, negotiated, and created *by* and *with* their peers. Professional learning communities can and must become the reform of this century with teachers as critical participants.

REFERENCES

Cochran-Smith, M., & S. Lytle. (1993). *Inside/outside: Teacher research and teacher knowledge.* New York: Teachers College Press.

Cochran-Smith, M., & Lytle, S. (2009). *Inquiry as stance: Practitioner research in the next generation.* New York: Teachers College Press.

Grossman, P., Wineburg, S., & Woolworth, S. (2001). Toward a theory of teacher community. *Teachers College Record, 103*(6), 942–1012.

Horn, I. S. (2005). Learning on the job: A situated account of teacher learning in high school mathematics departments. *Cognition and Instruction, 23*(2), 207–236.

Lieberman, A., & Miller, L. (2004). *Teacher leadership.* San Francisco: John Wiley & Sons.

Lieberman, A., & Miller, L. (2008). *Teachers in professional communities: Improving teaching and learning.* New York: Teachers College Press.

Lieberman, A., & Wood, D. R. (2002). *Inside the National Writing Project: Connecting network learning and classroom teaching.* New York: Teachers College Press.

Little, J. W., & Horn, I. S. (2007). "Normalizing" problems of practice: Converting routine conversation into a resource for learning in professional communities. In L. Stoll & K. S. Louis (Eds.), *Professional learning communities: Divergence, depth and dilemmas* (pp. 29–42). Maidenhead, UK: Open University Press.

Lortie, D. (1975). *Schoolteacher: A sociological study.* Chicago: University of Chicago Press.

McGuinn, P. (2010, June 18). *Divided democrats: The two narratives of school reform.* Retrieved from http://blogs.edweek.org/edweek/rick_ hess_straight_up/2010/06/divided_democrats_the_two_narratives_of_ school_reform.html

McLaughlin, M. W., & Talbert, J. E. (2001). *Professional communities and the work of high school teaching.* Chicago: University of Chicago Press.

McLaughlin, M. W., & Talbert, J. E. (2006). *Building school-based teacher learning communities: Professional strategies to improve student achievement.* New York: Teachers College Press.

National Commission on Excellence in Education. (1983). *A nation at risk: The imperative for educational reform.* Washington, DC: U.S. Government Printing Office.

Schon, D. A. (1983). *The reflective practitioner.* New York: Basic Books.

Talbert, J. (2010). Professional learning communities at the crossroads: How systems hinder or engender change. In A. Hargreaves et al. (Eds.), *Second international handbook of educational change* (pp. 555–572). New York: Springer.

Vesco, V., Ross, D., & Adams, A. (2008, January). A review of research on the impact of professional learning communities on teaching practice and student learning. *Teacher and Teacher Education, 24*(1), pp. 80–91.

Wenger, E. (1998). *Communities of practice: Learning, meaning, and identity.* Cambridge, UK: Cambridge University Press.

CHAPTER TWO

Creating Learning Communities

Shirley M. Hord and Patricia Roy

A ter a hearty breakfast, complemented with copious amounts of coffee, Dr. Kristin Willis, 4-year principal of Lincoln Middle School, met with the school's Mathematics Leadership Team (ML Team: Assistant Principal Joseph Lopez, Math Department Chair Clayton Washington, and the instructional coach for the math department, Mary Vaughn). Kristin thanked them for "maintaining the productivity of our school while I was in Chicago at an instructional learning conference for principals."

THE URGENT PROBLEM

"We've all been concerned about our lack of improved learning outcomes for our students. As we are all aware, the faculty cited the especially low performance of students in mathematics, and all agreed to address math across the curriculum in all subjects including phys ed and health education.

"We have provided a time and place for groups of all teachers in every academic department to meet; we've studied with them how to read multiple sources of student data; we've suggested a variety of new programs and practices to them and yet we are not seeing progress. What we have been doing is not working, we have all

19

agreed. So, we asked ourselves, what can we do, is there a new way to approach this problem?"

"Yes, it seems to me as I've said before, that our teachers are not really digging into the material that we have given them, even when we've reminded them that student state test scores must improve," Joe Lopez reported.

"Do you think that we may be on the wrong track by sending them to a two-day workshop where they get reams of stuff and then we expect their students to show improved results the next week . . . maybe they don't know how to use the new material, but an even more 'interesting' thought is whether they see the value or utility of some of their stacks of *What to Do to Improve Student Outcomes,*" Clayton remarked. "I have heard several of the teachers in the workroom sharing their discomfort and dismay about what 'all this stuff is' and whether it really addresses *their* students' learning needs."

"I am hearing similar mutterings," Mary shared, "when I sit with some of our teachers at lunch. They seem to feel 'out of the loop' and that someone, somewhere is dictating what they should do for their students, when this mysterious person has never been in their classrooms."

"Hm, yes, we've been hearing this, and we've unanimously agreed that we are in need of a new approach that will ensure that our teachers are committed to what will best serve students, and that they have a voice in determining what they should do in order that their students become more successful learners. We know that when individuals are involved in decisions, they are much more likely to act upon the decision. Does this make sense?" Kristin asked the group.

"Well, that might be a good idea, but where do we start on such ideas?" Joe impatiently inquired.

"It is a big ticket, Joe, but we've all agreed that we have an urgent problem and I think I may know where we can start. I've been reading some promising research about teachers working in a learning community and its impact on student outcomes (Vescio, Ross, and Adams, 2008, and Gallimore and Ermeling, 2010). I've also been collecting materials from the professional journals. One of the math teachers has been sharing information that her teaching sister in Santa Fe, Texas, has sent to her about a learning community in which she is engaged. I have brought multiple copies of handouts and materials that I collected at the conference that I just attended, and I have made a folder for each of us with all these materials—the journal articles, the research reports, the Texas teacher's information, and what I gained from the Chicago conference.

"We can begin by learning more about this learning community (LC) strategy/structure with this first paper that is about the six attributes or indicators of an effective learning community. Let me share a copy of this with you now, as an introduction." Principal Kristin added, "Take ten minutes to read this one-pager (from Hord & Tobia, 2012; Tobia & Hord, 2012), then take a ten-minute break, and we will chat about it."

When the team reconvened, "Wow," Clayton snorted, "this is some list. Is this possible and are all of these really necessary?" Mary noted that she had been reading about LCs and these notes were clearer, but she didn't understand all of them either.

"Let me see if I can explain," Kristin said. "You remember that in our discussions of improving our teaching so that our students learn better, we have said that we understand that *to improve,* we must discard ways of teaching that are not helping kids to learn and *change to* ways that have the potential to support their learning more effectively; but to do this, we must *learn* what the new way is and how to use it (see Figure 2.1). This means that improvement is based on changing, and changing is based on learning what the change is. The significant part of this is that the learning community's purpose is the learning of the professionals—thus, the learning community is the perfect context or environment in which to situate our improvement efforts."

"Oh, yes," Mary replied, "but this list of indicators looks daunting."

"It does, doesn't it," Kristin replied, "but we will take sufficient time to learn to do this, and we should remember that the faculty

Figure 2.1   A Sequence for Improvement

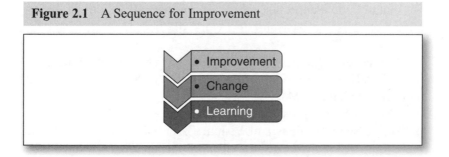

agreed for the math department to try a new approach to teaching math, and then help them all to understand and use it, for mathematics represents content knowledge, skills, critical thinking, problem solving, and reasoning, for starters, that are useful across all subjects and most certainly are needed after high school graduation/college.

"If you are willing, Mary and Clayton, we will do a pilot study first with your math teacher team to see if this works for this group and its students before extending it to the entire faculty."

"Well, we have talked and talked and read about this 'til I'm blue in the face, and now we are all a bit shaky about it, but fire ahead . . . I'll try to hang with you all, although I don't really understand why we need this learning community stuff," Joseph replied sullenly.

"Okay," Kristin responded, "let's refer to our list of six attributes and let me explain why each is required for the success of a learning community."

THE ATTRIBUTES OF PROFESSIONAL LEARNING COMMUNITIES: HOW DO MEMBERS OF A LEARNING COMMUNITY INTERACT AND WORK?

"First, please see Structural Conditions. It doesn't take rocket science to know that time, space, and other resources are necessary for people to come together in community, but this can impact the school's schedules, so we will need to give careful attention to this indicator. In discussion with the math team, we will need to consider how often the community should meet, where, when. Also, note the requirement for data. Fortunately, you all insisted that we have a large-scale series of learning sessions throughout last spring on how to read, understand, and interpret various sources of student data, so we should be in a good place there. If not, data study will be imperative, for it is the basis for the work of the community and for improvement."

"Yikes, and this is only for starters, but as you have noted, we have already accomplished a first step—that of learning to interpret and use data," noted Mary.

"Yes, that gives us a leg up. Now, let's look for a moment, please, at Shared Values and Vision. Essentially this vision is the target toward which we will be working—it is a mental image of the

Figure 2.2   Six Attributes of Learning Communities

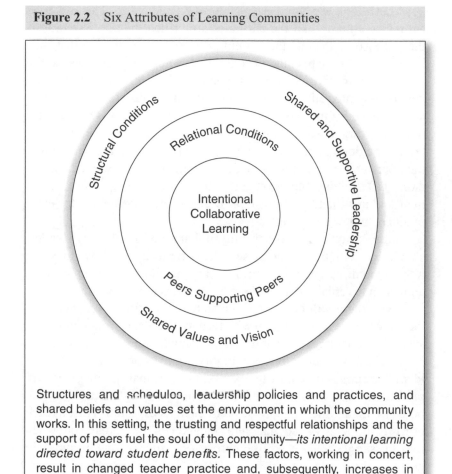

Structures and schedules, leadership policies and practices, and shared beliefs and values set the environment in which the community works. In this setting, the trusting and respectful relationships and the support of peers fuel the soul of the community—*its intentional learning directed toward student benefits.* These factors, working in concert, result in changed teacher practice and, subsequently, increases in student learning.

new 'way' that we have determined to use to improve our teaching so that students gain. It is foolish to start going somewhere if we don't know where we are going. Does this resonate?"

"Well," Clayton asked, "how do we do that?"

"We start by setting goals for the students' improved learning, and for ourselves, so that we are directing our energies to what students explicitly need for their successful learning. There is a tool that we can use to clarify where we are going . . . but we will learn about that in due time. Thanks for your question.

"Let's look at Shared and Supportive Leadership. This is a critical piece, although all the attributes are critical pieces. Not only is the purpose of the LC the learning of the participants so that they improve their practice and become more effective, but it is also the opportunity to give voice to its members. Giving staff a voice and developing into reliable decision makers and professionals cannot be accomplished if the state, or the district, or if I, or you, tell the communities what to do. That is like the hospital business administrator telling the doctors how to operate. It also means that the community members will, without question, have skills to be developed. Again, doing LC right is a big ticket and will require our help, support, and then taking a hands-off position to allow the community to learn, practice, and operate productively."

Joseph inquired, "Does this mean that all of us who have leadership roles will be losing those roles—figuring out how to share rather than directly guide the group? That would mean when to share and when to remain more 'in tune' with district and state directives?"

"Yes, there will be times when state and district parameters will dictate what we can do, so we will need to help the community understand the boundaries of their decision making. Does that make sense?

"Relational Conditions is a highly significant factor in the collaborative environment of the community, so that the members are productive. You can understand that respect and high regard for each other, no matter the 'wisdom' level of each, is essential. Trust in each other is imperative, so that individuals feel nonthreatened when making suggestions. It will be part of our role to support and help generate these relationships.

"Now, if you will look at Peers Supporting Peers, you will note an additional reason for the trust factor and other supportive relationships to be in place. If the LC is to be a self-organizing and self-governing body, and if the members are to make decisions about their learning, then they will turn to their peers to solicit and give feedback on their development of learning new practices. Principals at the conference told me that this attribute was the last to develop in the LC, and that is certainly easy to understand."

"And, I will venture to say that for peer teachers to leave their classrooms and visit another to do the peer observations, then scheduling to do that is another factor to care for—right?" asked Clayton.

"Yes, that is another nuts-and-bolts item—conditions, or infrastructure so to speak, but perhaps Mary can help here, or we will all figure it out. The last of the six attributes and the 'soul' of the LC is the matter of Intentional Collegial Learning. It is this part that is supported by and related to all other attributes. It is the purpose of the LC so that educators become continuing learners, teaching becomes of higher quality, and students learn more successfully . . . our goal for Lincoln Middle School."

"Stop right there, please. Do you think we can do all this? Really? How do we start?" asked Joseph pointedly.

"It does sound like a big challenge, and it is, for it is a different way and role for teachers and administrators to take. I suspect that if we had not seen this list, we could have identified much of the list as being reasonable factors that are required. We have the research literature to guide us; we have the reports of other schools that have accomplished this—although we must be aware that there are many schools claiming to be an LC that have not acquired all the attributes that are noted in the research. A number of the principals at the conference heartily agreed to serve as our consultants and share suggestions.

"We will be learning to operate as a learning community along with the pilot teachers. We will be taking these attributes on board as we are doing the job of a learning community. You might say that our acting in this new way will be learned through job-embedded professional learning.

"I have found two journal articles that will help us to identify explicitly our leadership team roles. Let me share copies with you. The ideas articulated by one article in *Educational Leadership* suggest that the principal's role in developing and supporting learning communities can be summarized as follows (Hord & Hirsh, 2009):

- Make clear to teachers that you know they can succeed—by working together
- Expect teachers to maintain a current knowledge base through continuous learning
- Guide the communities toward self-governance
- Provide data in accessible forms
- Instruct teachers in discussion and decision-making skills
- Share research results with teachers regularly
- Make time and effort to build trust
- Maintain a continuous orientation to student needs

"We can discuss these actions as we learn how to use our roles in developing learning communities in our school, for each of us will be supporting and promoting the development of learning communities across the school—and eventually, we should consider how to draw all the small-group learning communities into one larger one, so that we are all paddling the stream in the same direction. The second article (Hirsh & Hord, 2008) I will put in your mailboxes for review next week.

"Further, I understand that our superintendent has mentioned to a couple of school board members while on the golf course that we are looking into 'that LC business.' So we have much going for us—and expectations.

"In terms of how do we get started, our next meeting will give us the opportunity to study the cycle of continuous improvement that will serve as the frame to guide our LC work."

"Do you mean this is just school-improvement work? We know how to do that, although we haven't been doing a very fruitful job of it," Mary noted.

"Well, yes and no . . . it is school-improvement work, but with a difference. This difference is that the members of the LC engage in the steps of the cycle, determining their own way that will best benefit their students. This means a very different operation. When the community has gained adequate knowledge and skills and can conduct itself appropriately, then they lead their work and we step aside. We continue to support them and monitor their work, providing feedback as useful, but they have become independently functioning professionals—vastly rewarding to the members. Let's set a time for the cycle-of-improvement meeting on our calendars. I have a resource that explains the cycle—the work of the learning community. Please read this, mark it with questions or comments for our review together. We will schedule a second meeting that will focus on the knowledge and skills that the LC members will need and how we will accommodate that.

"It's been a longer meeting than I intended, colleagues, but I think we are on our way. It is natural to be shaky about starting something we haven't done before, so we will support each other. I am excited, and a bit nervous, but with you guys, anything is possible. Thanks for a productive meeting. On to the campus and our school day," concluded the principal.

Principal Kristin Willis and the team (Assistant Principal Joseph Lopez, Mathematics Chair Clayton Washington, Instructional Coach for the Mathematics Department Mary Vaughn) met on their appointed Saturday to discuss the various papers they had read and to plan steps for implementing the learning community structure/strategy in the math department, as a pilot test. They discussed and explored the seven steps of the cycle of continuous improvement, outlined by Learning Forward (2011). After exploring the lists of essential behaviors for each step in the cycle, they decided they would themselves become a learning team during the summer to understand more about each step. This study would allow all of them to provide assistance and support to the pilot team in using the cycle of continuous improvement over the course of the coming school year.

Kristin remarked, "I think that announcing to our teachers that we are now going to become a learning community is not a good idea. That will stimulate their concern and discomfort. Essentially, the learning community work is that of school improvement, which our teachers, and most teachers, are already obligated to do. The learning community, however, does its improvement work in a different way, and they will begin to see that as we support and guide them in this new 'model' of improving teaching and learning. We will support our pilot LC at every step of the way . . . giving a great deal of attention to the problems and practicalities of implementing the new practices that they will learn and put into place in their classrooms."

Assistant Principal Joseph Lopez and Mathematics Chair Clayton Washington met with individual members of the mathematics team to discuss their involvement in becoming a pilot learning team during the next school year. There was time set aside for questions and concerns that were noted and brought back to the leadership team for discussion. Joe and Clayton both emphasized that they were all going to be learning the process together and it would not involve merely working together—there were specific steps in the process that they would develop over the coming year.

Before the school term began in the fall, a special meeting was called with Kristin, the mathematics leadership team, and the school's mathematics department. An overview and summary of the seven-step cycle of continuous improvement was provided so that team members would have a vision of the process. Jointly, they decided to build their knowledge and skills throughout the school year while simultaneously learning how to become a learning community.

In mentally reviewing what she had learned at the conference and in her reading, Kristin was holding tightly onto her notes about the significant role of the principal and leadership team. This learning and leading team, she was discovering, was very important in developing an LC. There was guidance to be provided at the outset, but then it was necessary to relinquish the reins so that teachers could become self-organizing and have a voice to make decisions—within school and district parameters, of course. Supporting the communities in developing a clear and specific vision of where they were headed, once they made a decision for a new method of instruction, they would need to consider how well, across time, they were achieving their goals for students. Kristin could now understand better just what function each of the indicators of an LC really meant and why they were important. It became readily apparent to her that she had a large role to play in supporting the staff in developing departmental LCs and preparing them to participate productively. She began to make a mental list of the knowledge, skills, and dispositions that staff would need: reviewing and interpreting multiple sources of student data; communicating meaningfully; working and learning collaboratively; using conflict resolution in contentious situations; selecting decision-making models; and developing attitudes of respect and regard for their fellow community members, as well as trust and trustworthiness . . . to mention the most obvious.

Ah, there was much work to be done. Kristin was certain that students could become much more successful learners if their teachers also believed this and committed themselves to this goal—the goal to which the Mathematics Learning and Leadership Team is committed.

The next section provides a description of each step of the cycle of continuous improvement along with tools and strategies useful for each phase. Following each description, the story of the pilot mathematics learning team is shared—how they learned to become a learning community and how they learned to use the cycle of continuous improvement in their learning community.

THE CYCLE OF CONTINUOUS IMPROVEMENT: WHAT DO MEMBERS OF A LEARNING COMMUNITY DO?

The seven-step cycle of continuous improvement is found in Figure 2.3. Underlying this cycle is the belief that as educator knowledge and skills strengthen, students will benefit and learn at higher levels. The cycle begins with an examination of student learning needs and identification of student learning goals. Then the learning community identifies the knowledge and skills educators need to attain the student learning goal. The cycle also involves identifying how to support the implementation of those new skills and practices in the classroom and how to evaluate the impact of new practices on student learning.

This cycle makes a direct connection between student and educator learning needs. To be effective, it will require educators to develop and use new norms of operation and effective interactional knowledge, skills, and processes. The remainder of this section will explain each step in more detail.

Figure 2.3   Cycle of Continuous Improvement

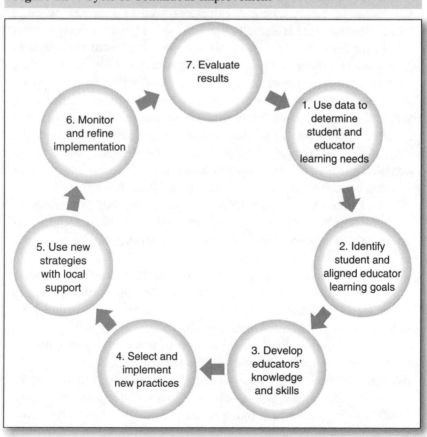

Source: Learning Forward, 2011.

Step 1: Use Data to Determine
Student and Educator Learning Needs

In the last 10 years, educators have become more comfortable with analyzing classroom and achievement data to determine student learning needs. Most have also become skillful at identifying curricular needs based on student learning outcomes. Many have not yet taken the next step to identify their own learning needs based on what students need. This step requires two specific components: (1) identifying, through the analysis of a variety of student learning data, student learning needs and (2) identifying educator learning needs required to attain identified student learning needs.

For example, an analysis of student data might show that students are not being successful with items that use higher-order questions on the district interim assessment. Educators need to determine whether that student outcome is a result of an absence of higher-order questions within current curriculum materials, inappropriate instructional strategies, a need for more wait time during instruction, or instructors needing to learn more about the use of instructional scaffolding, which supports students to learn how to answer these new types of questions. Someone within the learning community might have the solution; it could also require LC members to conduct an online search to learn about the myriad possible solutions to address this student learning issue. It is a complex instructional and curricular issue that will necessitate educator learning and implementing new instructional practices.

A framework called a KASAB can make the professional learning targets more tangible by identifying the specific learning outcomes (Killion, 2008). Educator learning outcomes can be organized into five categories (see Table 2.1).

An educator learning goal, focused on the use of higher-order questions, could be categorized into the components shown in Table 2.2. This delineation can help team members determine what to learn about and identify practices they will commit to implement.

One of the most challenging aspects of this analysis and diagnosis will be that each educator within the learning community will have to examine his/her own level of knowledge and skills and be willing to share that self-assessment with colleagues. For most adults, sharing strengths is much easier than sharing needs. As a consequence, one of the essential interactional norms for the LC will be to develop trust. Trust is the ability to be open and honest while expecting others to be open, honest, and trustworthy. Trust involves

Table 2.1   KASAB Framework

	Definition	*Example*
Knowledge	Conceptual understanding of information, theories, principles and research	• Knowledge of how students develop conceptual knowledge • Knowledge of the components of differentiated instruction
Attitude	Beliefs about the value of particular information or strategies	• Belief that all students can learn when given enough time and support • Belief that peer collaboration is essential for educator learning
Skills	Strategies and processes to apply knowledge	• How to develop differentiated instruction • How to plan lessons that align with student learning standards and level of knowledge
Aspirations	Desires or internal motivation to engage in a particular practice	• A desire to support students who struggle with learning • A desire to collaborate with colleagues to improve instructional practices in the building
Behavior	Consistent application/use of developed knowledge and skills	• Consistent use of graphic organizers during instruction • Consistent use of differentiated instruction

Source: Killion, 2008. Used with permission.

risk, in this case, the risk that members of the LC might share each person's self-assessment with people outside the team. Team member confidentiality is critical for a well-functioning learning community.

For Step 1, an effective learning community will

- analyze a variety of student achievement data, including standardized tests, interim assessments, and classroom work using rubrics
- identify specific knowledge and skills that students require to improve achievement results
- identify priority student learning needs

(Continued)

> (Continued)
> - identify educator learning needs based on research, best practice, educator standards, and member knowledge
> - identify each teacher's own learning needs related to student learning needs
> - develop trusting relationships among learning community membership

Table 2.2   Sample KASAB

Knowledge *Know . . .*	- Knowledge of different types of higher-level questions - Knowledge of how to analyze questions within curricular materials to determine appropriateness - Knowledge of how to develop appropriate higher-level questions matched to student learning outcomes - Knowledge about instructional scaffolding
Attitude *Believe that . . .*	- All students can learn to answer higher-level questions - Teachers can support all students to answer higher-level questions - Instructional scaffolding is essential to help all students answer higher-level questions
Skills *Can . . .*	- Use wait time during instruction - Analyze and identify levels of existing questions within curricular materials - Develop additional higher-level questions for existing curricular units - Develop new curricular materials that include higher-level questions matching student learning outcomes - Develop instructional scaffolding skills
Aspirations *Desires to . . .*	- A desire to use wait time during instruction and small-group work to encourage student engagement - A desire to use instructional scaffolding to support learning of *all* students, especially those who struggle
Behaviors *Consistently uses . . .*	- Higher-level questions during instruction - Wait time during instruction - Support for all students to answer higher-level questions - Instructional scaffolding to support all students to answer higher-level questions

Source: Killion, 2008. Used with permission.

This Step in Action: During the previous school year, the Lincoln Middle School faculty had engaged in six sessions to learn how to review, analyze, understand, and interpret student learning results. Most teachers were comfortable with the process but welcomed a well-defined structure to follow. Assistant Principal Joe Lopez made certain that the tables of student results were reconfigured into colorful charts and graphs, making the data easier to read and analyze.

Clayton, the mathematics chair, and Mary, the mathematics coach, met with the pilot math LC to explore their available achievement data. This group of math teachers and the two facilitators compiled a wide array of student data: disaggregated state assessment results, final district interim scores from the year before, and student demographic data.

> The learning community is addressing the structural conditions, one of the factors required for a learning community.

Collaboratively, the group established, after soliciting Joe's help for space and scheduling, a regular weekly time and place to meet for learning and using the cycle of continuous improvement. This first meeting focused on data review, analysis, and interpretation about what to do to address students' low performance areas as well as identifying student strengths and areas of growth.

One area stood out starkly—the gap in scores between white students and African-American and Hispanic students. The disaggregated results illustrated that this was a historic gap that began in elementary grades and became even wider at middle school. Student learning needs encompassed even the most basic knowledge and skills as well as mathematical practices. Yet functions and algebraic thinking were highlighted as essential needs. The team decided they needed to figure out what strategies they could use to close the gap. The Common Core standards, which the state and district were in process of adopting, included much more rigorous outcomes in middle schools for the "expressions and equations" domain. With Clayton and Mary's support, the team decided they would explore the teaching practices included in this domain for their relevance to their students' needs. They also thought they might need to explore how to deepen the content they focused on during instruction.

> Note that another of the six attributes is beginning to show itself—that of shared and supportive leadership; Mary and Clayton do not *tell* the teachers what to do but engage them in group decision making, thus modeling collaborative work and providing opportunities for group sharing of power, authority, and making decisions—leadership actions.

This first step launched their LC's use of data to improve instruction based on students' needs.

They struggled in defining their learning needs using the KASAB format. Learning community members were familiar with identifying student learning needs but not how to identify their own learning needs related to student needs. Initially, they decided that they needed to develop:

- **K**nowledge: Knowledge of the expressions and equations domain and knowledge of instructional strategies that addressed classroom equity, knowledge of how students learn functions, and algebraic thinking
- **A**ttitudes: A belief that *all* students would learn more rigorous mathematics when teachers changed their instructional practices
- **S**kills: How to adjust instruction to engage all students in mathematical reasoning; how to adjust instructional materials to support an equitable classroom
- **A**spiration: The group couldn't identify any aspirations
- **B**ehaviors: Consistent use of new instructional materials about functions and algebraic thinking; consistent use of student engagement strategies

Step 2: Identify Student and Aligned Educator Learning Goals

This step contains three components: (1) identify goals that reflect student learning needs; subsequently, (2) specify goals for educators that address the learning needs of students, and (3) identify strategies and practices to accomplish those goals.

Many educators have become skillful at writing student learning goals in a SMART goal format. SMART stands for **S**: strategic/specific, **M**: measurable, **A**: attainable, **R**: results oriented, and **T**: time bound. A student learning goal might be stated as, "In 3 years, all third-grade students will read at grade level or better as measured by the district's benchmark assessment." It is *specific* because it identifies third-grade students and the attainment of the grade-level reading benchmarks. It is *measurable* because it states that the district's benchmark test will be used to determine whether the goal has been achieved. It is *attainable* because it allows 3 years to reach the goal. It is *results* *oriented* because success is all students being able to read at grade level. It is *time bound* because it is expected to be accomplished within 3 years.

While creating SMART goals for student learning might be familiar, developing a

A brief description of each of the components of a SMART goal is provided in Resource A (page 79). If the reader is unfamiliar with the components of a SMART goal, it will be a useful resource. It also provides examples that can help when developing student and educator impact goals.

SMART goal for educator learning might be novel for many educators. In many schools and districts, professional learning is an activity and not a goal with specific outcomes or results. In many districts and schools, the connection between professional learning and student learning is not always apparent. Unfortunately, in many places, professional learning still involves hours spent in training or workshops and not in the development of specific knowledge, skills, and practices that provide solutions to student learning challenges. Making the connection between student needs and educator learning is crucial so that staff members understand that their learning has a direct impact on student learning.

A SMART goal that makes the connection between educator and student learning might be stated as, "Classroom teachers will learn and consistently implement, with quality, instructional strategies that improve word decoding skills so that fourth-grade students will read at grade level or better as measured by the district's benchmark assessment. Within 2 years, teachers will consistently use identified instructional strategies and the level of quality implementation will be measured by a descriptive practice profile or innovation configuration map."

When learning community members are involved in analyzing and identifying the relationship between student and educator learning needs, they are much more likely to develop ownership and commitment to attaining the goals. SMART educator learning goals are compelling and involve a level of accountability that many educators may be unaccustomed to realizing. Educators are more likely to accept the responsibility when they are involved in identifying the skills and practices, writing the goals, and establishing the connection between their learning and student success. They might be less willing to commit to a goal if it has been established by others outside the LC.

The learning community members also need to search for strategies, instructional practices, and content knowledge that correspond with the educator learning goal. First, LC members should canvas their own knowledge bases and practices to determine whether someone within the team or school has demonstrated success in the same area of student learning on which they are focused. Sometimes the answer lies within the school community, and student learning data will be able to support that accomplishment. Tapping expertise of specialists within the district and region is also useful.

If no evidence of improved student learning exists within the LC, the school, or the district, members will need to begin a search for viable strategies and practices that focus specifically on student learning needs in their target area. This requires LC members to become critical consumers of research. This is an important step that the LC must not skip because of either urgency or enthusiasm. The temptation is to identify a strategy or practice used by another school or district without ensuring it supports their students' needs and learning goals.

Many Internet-based clearinghouse databases are now available through the Institute of Education Sciences (http://ies.ed.gov/) and the What Works Clearinghouse, which collects, screens, and identifies studies of educational intervention programs such as beginning reading, dropout prevention, mathematics, literacy, science, and English language learners (http://ies.ed.gov/ncee/wwc/). The ERIC network also catalogues, summarizes, and provides access to a variety of educational topics such as reading, English, science, mathematics, disabilities, and gifted education (www.eric.ed.gov). These clearinghouses provide information about practices and their effectiveness in improving student learning.

Essential questions for the LC to answer at this point include the following:

- What evidence of student achievement is available? Is it specific enough to address the student needs you have identified?
- Did the research include students with demographics similar to your population (socioeconomic status [SES], ethnicity, special education, or type of school)?
- Was there information about what educators needed to know and be able to do to improve student learning?

- Did the educator practices identify both content knowledge and instructional strategies?
- Are there any descriptions of the professional learning processes used to develop educator knowledge and skills?
- Are there clear descriptions of the new practice in operation (innovation configuration maps, look fors, or rubrics)?

Once this information has been collected, the team should review the evidence and identify the strategies that have demonstrated improvement in their focus area. The LC is charged with making the decision about appropriate strategies to adopt. This is an aspect of the shared leadership attribute that provides an opportunity for LC members to not only identify student needs but also identify the solutions that educators will adopt to address those needs.

At first, LC members might need the assistance of an instructional coach or school administrator to facilitate the decision-making process. Making this kind of shared and binding decision is uncommon in many school environments in which classroom work remains a solo endeavor. Unless the LC has developed a strong level of trust, clear communication patterns, use of conflict-management strategies, and the appropriate use of dialogue, LC members might need assistance to make a decision and follow through on transforming classroom practices.

In Step 2, an effective learning community will

- develop student learning goal/s using a SMART goal format
- develop educator learning goal/s that align with student learning needs
- develop educator learning goal/s in the SMART goal format
- identify evidence-based strategies that improve student learning
- make a shared decision to adopt and use identified strategies

A more in-depth description of this step can be found in the Data volume within this series.

This Step in Action: Even with Clayton's facilitation, creating educator learning goals was difficult for the LC. It was easy for them to establish the student learning goal in a SMART goal format. But the team struggled, disagreed, and strained when it came to identifying a SMART goal for their own learning. During these debates, Clayton

> Wisely, Clayton is teaching the community to use conflict-solving strategies—another skill required for the LC (Johnson & Johnson, 2011).

introduced them to conflict-management strategies and shared with them a process to use, followed by providing opportunities for them to practice the process. The math team recognized the need for conflict-management skills so that they could productively share their ideas, since frequently some individuals' ideas were very different from those of the majority of the teachers.

The idea of learning goals for teachers was a new concept for them. Professional learning usually didn't involve a commitment to follow through and use new strategies in the classroom. That implication stunted their thinking and short-circuited creative thought. After an initial disappointingly unsuccessful meeting on this topic, Clayton decided to confer with the school's leadership team.

At this meeting of Principal Kristin, AP Joe, Clayton, and Mary, the dilemma was described and the group pondered it. After some reflection, Joe tentatively asked, "Some time back, someone suggested a tool that would help everyone to understand and to see more clearly—to clarify, I think—what the new way of teaching math would look like, something called innovation configurations, I believe. I don't recall the details, but I wonder if we could learn more about it, and if it would help us to be able to identify the teacher's role in the classroom, and obviously, the goal(s) that we and the teachers identify and that we will pursue and support them in achieving . . . hm? I think I am correct in thinking that this would also help us with one of the LC indicators, that of shared vision, that is, everyone having a shared mental picture of what our new math strategies should look like when they are in the classroom, implemented in a high-quality way . . . what do you think about that?"

"Good idea, Joe. And that reminds me that Mary and Clayton visited with the math specialist at the regional educational service center some time back and the subject of innovation configurations came up. Remind us about that," requested Kristin.

"Oh, yes," Mary responded, "we had a 2-hour, very productive meeting with Mike Jones, who is known to be an expert on this matter of what do teachers need to know and do—learning goals for teachers—in order to address identified student goals. And he said that he could help us, and that, further, at the high school at the other end of town, the math head is experienced with helping math teachers to learn new skills, and Mike was certain that we could find assistance there, and that he could help us in learning about the innovation configuration maps that Joe was alluding to."

"Yeah," Clayton added, "Mike put it all into a larger context by commenting on the way the United States seems to go about school change and improvement, contrasted with western European countries, which commit up to 10 years for a large-scale change and supply on-site facilitators to help teachers learn new strategies, and facilitate and support them in implementation. He suggested that the United States is like a microwave society when improving schools—we quickly snatch a new practice or process, pop it into the oven for 4 minutes, and voila! It is done, and we move on to something else. He suggested that we are so eager to act, that rather than invest in the time to carefully articulate where we are going, via goals, we rush into actions that we mistake for goals. That made sense to me and resonates with what I am seeing and hearing as we work for mathematics improvement for our students. It helps me begin to understand how we might address our current challenge of teachers' learning goals."

Kristin added, "It's probably a good idea to ask our director of professional learning to work with us so that we make sure that our administrators' and teachers' learning experiences are not superficial but are truly effective. I believe we are moving very productively along our journey to improved teacher mathematics effectiveness and subsequently to increased student mathematics learning. Everyone has contributed so meaningfully to this effort. Big thanks for our progress so far."

Subsequent to these interactions, a day-long learning session with Mike Jones and the math department head at the other high school, Crystal Lana, and two meetings with the math team facilitated by Clayton and Mary (with Joe stopping in on one meeting for a short time to observe), the math teachers came to some conclusions about goals. The LC decided that the first round of educator SMART goals had to be smaller and more manageable. The SMART goal for student and educator learning that the team created and agreed upon stated:

Seventh- and eighth-grade mathematics teachers will learn and consistently implement instructional strategies that improve functions and algebraic thinking so that the achievement gap between white and Hispanic/African-American students is reduced by 8% or better as measured by the district's bench-mark assessment and the annual state assessment.

Step 3: Develop Educators' Knowledge and Skills

Step 3 focuses on educators engaging in professional learning in order to extend their knowledge and skills regarding new practices, content, content-specific pedagogy, how students learn, and management of classroom environments that support solutions to students' learning needs.

Many educators report that their typical professional learning involves watching a video clip of a new instructional practice. The video clip might take place at a different grade level or in a different content area than that of the teachers who are viewing it, yet once they have watched this demonstration, they are expected to employ that new practice with their students.

Experts in the field of professional learning don't believe that experience is sufficient for changing instructional behavior. Bruce Joyce and Emily Calhoun's (2010) study of professional development suggests that there are several components that need to be planned and executed when a new curriculum or instructional practice is introduced. First, knowledge of new content and understanding student learning outcomes is essential. This knowledge is not casual; it needs to be deeply understood—at teachers' fingertips—so they can use it with ease when planning courses, units of study, and individual lessons. Principals, assistants, and instructional coaches also need to understand content and the depth of knowledge involved in new student learning outcomes in order to provide appropriate feedback and assistance for instruction.

In addition, other topics might include content-specific pedagogy, how students of different ages or learning styles learn new information, differentiated instruction strategies, and classroom management techniques, especially if students are expected to learn collaboratively with their peers. Developing the knowledge base includes understanding (1) components parts, (2) critical attributes, (3) underlying theory, and (4) when to use or *not* use specific strategies. Even though many educators might want to jump to learning new strategies first, knowledge provides the foundation for the effective use of new strategies and the development of professional decision making (Joyce & Calhoun, 2010; Marzano, Pickering, & Pollock, 2001).

Step 3 also involves developing new instructional skills. New instructional strategies are also built through understanding essential components and critical attributes. Demonstrations play an important role in learning to use new strategies, but study in this area suggests that at least 20 or more demonstrations are needed over the course of a year to build new practices. These examples can be accomplished through demonstration lessons conducted by instructional coaches, outside experts, or expert team members, observations of a master teacher, or videos. To be used most effectively, observations and demonstrations require additional investigations: labeling the essential components, collaborative discussions, and analysis of strengths and barriers.

A third component, required for development of new skills, involves planning and preparation. New curriculum and student learning outcomes will require the use of different instructional strategies. Some of these strategies are material intensive. If inquiry is required to ensure students understand the scientific method, everything from balances, magnets, and computer software to worms and frogs might be needed for instruction. Teachers will need time to collect essential materials and also to plan, practice, and refine lessons and units of instruction. "Teachers need to reach the classroom with lessons in hand, complete with the materials they will use" (Joyce & Calhoun, 2010, p. 77).

Huge amounts of practice, feedback, and refinement are required when new curriculum and instruction are initiated. A more complex change requires more time than would refining current curriculum or instructional methods. Practice of new skills needs to occur consistently over months before we could expect educators to master new curriculum and instructional processes. Educator learning communities play a critical role in providing the platform for this practice, feedback, and refinement. As teachers learn about new content and instructional practices, they can plan new lessons and strategies collectively, practice in the classroom while being observed by a peer, process collegial feedback with peers, and refine the lesson plan collaboratively with other team members.

In Step 3, an effective learning community will

- develop a knowledge base aligned with educator's learning goals
- develop skills corresponding to educators' learning goals
- identify professional learning designs that will support their learning

A more in-depth description of this step can be found in the Learning Design volume within this series.

This Step in Action: The pilot math LC decided to begin their learning by focusing on the instructional shifts, a fundamental principle of the Common Core mathematics standards. One of the differences within the new standards was an emphasis on rigor. Rigor emphasized a three-pronged pursuit of conceptual understanding, procedural skill and fluency, and application. This was quite a shift from the expectations of past mathematics standards. The professional learning director, Dominique Garcia, who had joined their meeting, indicated she could provide the LC with a set of materials about the instructional shifts inherent in the Common Core mathematics standards. The group decided to divide up the materials and share with each other what they had learned. That grounding in the assumptions that undergird the new standards took a number of weeks to accomplish. They were challenged by the new expectations and wondered whether their students were up to it.

Mary, with assistance from Dominique, also provided a set of instructional videos for the math group to view. Mary suggested a structure in which the group would identify and label the essential components of the instructional strategy; hold collaborative discussions on lesson design, student learning outcomes, and student behaviors; and analyze the strengths and obstacles within the lesson. An observation that came from their reflection on the videos was the amount of time that students talked with each other during the lesson. The team began to see this as a significantly different strategy from the way they typically taught mathematics.

The team, again with Mary's help, did an online search for exemplary lessons that focused on the instructional shifts they had been reading about. The LC members dissected each lesson, especially focusing on whether all students were involved during instruction.

Step 4: Select and Implement New Practices

Step 4 focuses on selecting and implementing appropriate evidence-based strategies (new practices) to achieve educator learning goals and, consequently, student learning goals.

A major consideration for the LC will be to identify strategies, processes, and learning designs to help and support each team member to implement these new strategies. The transition from knowing about a new strategy to actually using that strategy with quality and agility is difficult. This has been called the knowing–doing gap (Pfeffer & Sutton, 2000), and it exists in all walks of life. There is a wide gulf between knowing about a new practice and actually putting that practice into operation on a consistent basis. Creating a new habit is complicated; for most adults this involves eliminating a current practice and replacing it with a new one. Most adults need support, assistance, and attention to take a new set of behaviors and transform them into a natural routine. This reality might explain the existence of a myriad of support groups for everything from weight control to grief counseling.

Collaborative professional learning strategies, which support the use of new practices, are necessary. While workshops and training build the knowledge base, collaborative work within the LC is required to ensure teachers apply their new knowledge daily to lesson and unit development and receive ongoing support and assistance in implementing new strategies. Collaborative strategies necessitate developing productive relationships among colleagues so that they can learn from and with each other to enhance their own skills and incorporate new practices to improve student learning. This kind of shared decision making, along with collegial assistance and support, is a building block for collective responsibility among LC members. Collective responsibility entails peer accountability for improving student learning undergirded by support that team members commit to each other to accomplish the goal collaboratively.

Some collaborative professional learning strategies that can support implementation include the following:

- **Peer observations:** A structured visit between colleagues in which the visiting teacher can view the use of a new strategy or become another set of eyes and ears for the classroom teacher, observing student and teacher behaviors and engaging in a debriefing with the classroom teacher. A plan for the observation is created and specific teacher and student behaviors are agreed upon before the visit (peers supporting peers condition) (Lock, 2006; Killion, 2011).
- **Coplanning:** Teams of teachers or a teacher working with a coach develop a lesson using new content, instructional practices, or assessment strategies. The purpose is to think

through the use of new strategies and determine how the educator can put them into practice in the classroom. The planning phase has been recognized as an important step in preparing to use new strategies in the classroom.

- **Coteaching:** A logical next step to codeveloping a lesson is to use that lesson in the classroom, coteaching with a colleague or coach. Having two people in the classroom allows each person to watch how students are reacting, what unexpected challenges occurred, and whether the content and process were appropriate. A debriefing follows the lesson to identify strengths, needs, refinements, and revisions.
- **Demonstration lessons:** Early in the process of adopting and using new strategies, educators need a strong, positive example of how to use those strategies in their own content area and with their own students. An expert colleague or coach provides a model lesson in the teacher's classroom. Frequently, the coach or colleague plans the lesson in collaboration with the teacher. It is important that critical attributes of the strategy are identified and used during observation and during a debriefing of the lesson. This real-life example can solidify educators' vision of the strategy in practice.
- **Lesson study:** This seven-step process to learn how to improve student learning is focused on what students are learning rather than on what teachers plan to teach. It involves the following:
  - o forming a team of teachers who work together
  - o identifying an area of mutual focus, many times an area of high-priority need
  - o planning a lesson collaboratively with attention to how students might respond to different aspects of the lesson
  - o preparing observation processes and procedures
  - o teaching and observing a lesson—collecting observational data
  - o debriefing the lesson
  - o planning for next steps (Richardson, 2004)
- **Constructing and scoring assessments:** Assessments are used to measure student learning; teachers work together to develop assessments to measure learning of new standards. Together colleagues learn about assessments by developing, administering, and scoring common assessments. The collaborative

development helps educators to clarify their expectations for students, identify quality work, refine their understanding of student content standards, and enlarge their repertoire of assessment strategies (McTighe & Emberger, 2006).

- **Analyzing student work:** Examining student work in collaboration with other colleagues helps educators focus on what students are learning in light of what the teachers asked them to accomplish. The analysis can identify what students know, student confusion, student misunderstanding, and the level of cognitive processing accomplished by students. Many protocols can help structure this conversation so that it is productive and respectful of the educator who shares student work (Richardson, 2001).

In Step 4, an effective learning community will

- identify and use evidence-based professional learning strategies that improve educator learning
- identify collaborative professional learning strategies that support each other's implementation of new practices
- plan for ongoing practice, feedback, and refinement of new skills

A more in-depth description of strategies can be found in the Implementation volume within this series.

This Step in Action: In the midst of their conversations, dialogues, and discussions about the new mathematics standards and the necessity of instructional rigor, math team member Brian Long found a list of criteria defining student engagement during instruction. Most of the LC members were astonished by the list; it did not match their definition of student engagement. Mario, an LC member, suggested that student engagement might be a fruitful area of study and focus for the LC. Because they listened carefully to understand each other's ideas and perspectives, they were able to come to a consensus that the LC would focus on student engagement.

Another indicator of LC—the community identifying what their members will continuously, intentionally, and collegially learn to increase their effectiveness with students.

Student engagement involved giving voice to all students, creating opportunities for students to share their thinking, and scaffolding learning activities so that those students who rarely participated in class became contributing members. Nikki, another LC member, remarked to the team, "You know, giving voice to students seems like a reflection of our process of working together as a group in our increasing collaborative learning and planning."

They decided to explore a series of lesson vignettes to identify two things: (1) what student participation strategies were used and (2) what mathematics lesson materials and processes were used. The LC identified, recorded, and discussed the properties of both aspects of student engagement. Next, the LC decided to focus on a set of cluster standards that all of them would be using during the next unit. Each person took a lesson, transformed the instructional materials, and identified student engagement strategies. These plans were brought back and discussed, reviewed, and revised by the LC. Mary, their mathematics coach, was invited to participate in this discussion. Her experience and feedback helped them identify strengths and weaknesses in their plans. They decided to do another round of revisions before using the plans.

With Mary's assistance, they coplanned a demonstration lesson in which Mary modeled how to introduce the new engagement strategy to students. They began with a simple strategy: pairing up and sharing student reasoning, sometimes referred to "A talks and B listens." They realized that this strategy also required reconfiguring the instructional materials so that students were not merely following an algorithm but were allowed to think about a variety of approaches to solving problems. The LC members realized that this strategy required developing deeper knowledge and skills about restructuring the lessons rather than merely giving students time to talk. Student talk and reasoning had to focus on the Common Core instructional shifts.

Assistant Principal Joe helped rearrange schedules so they could all observe the demonstration lesson (structural conditions). Mary modeled how to introduce the "A talks and B listens" but also set norms for *how* students would talk with each other. She demonstrated acceptable and unacceptable conversations that would be used in this activity. A lot of the examples had to do with paying attention to what the other person was saying, making eye contact, and engaging in active listening.

After the demonstration lesson, each LC member planned to take one class and conduct the same lesson. They paired up and asked their partners to be another set of eyes and ears during the lesson. At the end of the day, they shared their observations, identified strengths, and identified ways to refine the approach.

> The LC is beginning to learn about peers supporting peers, an LC attribute.

LC members continued to practice this single strategy until it felt comfortable and became a familiar routine in the classroom. They continued to discuss how students were responding to the new strategies and whether there were any discernible changes in student learning or attitude. One of the team's insights was that curriculum reconfiguration was much more difficult than the use of engagement strategies, and they revised their learning goal to include reconfiguring their mathematics curriculum.

"The math community is very stimulated and making significant progress in planning, preparing, and practicing their developing mathematics knowledge and skills in teaching the 'new' math," Kristin shared with the leadership team early in January at their regular weekly meeting in which they shared observations and opinions about the pilot math team's efforts. "The team is developing great skills using the cycle of continuous improvement. I wonder exactly where they stand in terms of working as an LC. I found an IC map of effective, research-based learning communities and I'm wondering if we might use it to assess progress of our work with them to develop as an LC."

"Hey, that's an idea! While using it in this way, we would become familiar with this tool and could make more informed decisions about trying to create and use our own map for the new

> Resource B (page 83) is a copy of the innovation configuration (IC) map of learning communities. One of the uses of an IC map is to use it as a self-assessment instrument. Ask each member of an LC to rate her or his current behaviors using the IC map. The LC as a whole examines the results and identifies areas of strength and areas for improvement. Based on these results, they make a plan to improve their interactions and work.

math practices that the teachers are studying and trying to incorporate in their classroom instruction," Mary remarked.

"I will make copies of the IC map of LCs and place them in your mail slots, and next meeting we can discuss them and possibly prepare to use the IC to assess where the team is, related to strong performance as an LC, and where they may need assistance."

Step 5: Use New Strategies With Local Support

The need for ongoing practice, feedback, and application of learning was addressed in the third step of this cycle. Research by Bruce Joyce and Beverly Showers (cited in Joyce & Calhoun, 2010) found that when traditional training activities are used to develop teacher knowledge and skills, long-term implementation typically does not occur. They found only 10% of teachers learned the skills well enough to integrate them as one of their routine teaching strategies (Joyce & Calhoun, 2010). Professional learning focused on long-term use of new practices includes (1) study of the underlying rationale for the use of new instruction, plus (2) multiple demonstrations of the strategies in practice, plus (3) planning for the use of new strategies in lessons and units, and (4) implementation supplemented with regular peer coaching. When all four components are employed, more than 90% of teachers studied attained long-term use of new curricular and instructional strategies. Joyce and Calhoun's (2010) findings concluded that teachers are quite capable of learning new strategies if professional learning is organized, planned, and implemented including those four elements.

The use of instructional coaches is one beneficial support strategy to assist teachers as they learn to use new practices in the classroom. Coaches' roles are multifaceted. Instructional coaches need to be able to

- build the educator's knowledge base of content and instruction,
- provide demonstration lessons and conduct debriefings,
- provide resources,
- facilitate problem-solving sessions,
- reinforce collaborative interaction among learning communities,
- analyze student and educator data,
- collect formative assessment data on teacher learning, and
- do it all with a smile!

Obviously, a single coach cannot fulfill the needs of an entire school, but the good news is that research has shown that LC members can provide much of the same support and assistance to each other. The LC identifies members' learning needs, learns together, plans lessons collaboratively, reviews student work and results, identifies refinements to the lessons, and examines progress being made by teachers and students.

Many structured formats and procedures have been developed by McDonald and the Coalition of Essential Schools to facilitate these collaborative conversations and discussions (McDonald, Mohr, Dichter, & McDonald, 2007; http://www.nsrfharmony.org/protocol/a_z.html). The structured and timed interactions, or protocols, ensure that everyone has a chance to talk and to listen, that conversation is not dominated by a single person, and that deep and thoughtful dialogue occurs within a circumscribed time frame.

Sufficient time is required for teachers to learn about new strategies and then practice their use in the classroom. Two to 3 years of ongoing support may be required to ensure that high-quality implementation of new strategies is accomplished by a majority of the faculty. A complex change involving new student learning standards, new curriculum and corresponding instructional practices, new assessment strategies, and intricate collaborative interactions among staff members will take even longer. Research in this area suggests the time frame would be upward of 5 years.

In Step 5, an effective learning community will

- collaboratively plan lessons
- create multiple opportunities for members to practice new skills and strategies, give and receive feedback, and refine their practice with peer collaboration
- collect classroom observational data
- provide feedback
- refine current lesson and classroom practices based on feedback

This Step in Action: The math LC decided that they would conduct another round of learning about new engagement strategies, practice the new strategies with the assistance of a partner, and collect and analyze student reactions and classroom test results. They were buoyed by their success and decided to up the ante and schedule demonstration lessons. These demos were provided by the "partners" for the rest of the team. The district coach, Mary, agreed to provide coaching assistance to each partnership, collect observation data of teachers and students, and provide feedback about strengths and limitations of the lesson. If these demonstrations went well, they planned to offer them to other staff members during a school-wide professional learning day.

The math LC also continues to reconfigure lesson materials, shares those plans, and discusses the strengths and limitations of the lessons using the tuning protocol. The tuning protocol is a timed, seven-step process that structures a discussion among colleagues (Richardson, 2001). The focus is defined by one of the members, who asks a question on which he/she wants feedback and thinking from the group. Each LC member has a turn as the focusing teacher.

Kristin brought a special treat for the learning community to celebrate their progress. The data the leadership team collected during classroom walk-throughs showed students were more actively engaged during mathematics instruction. The community was now ready to create a more refined goal to increase the number of active engagement strategies used in their classrooms and continued to work with Clayton and Mary to reconfigure instructional materials to allow more opportunities for students to think out loud about their mathematical reasoning.

The team decided to deepen their understanding of the expressions and equations domain. Adjusting content materials to encourage and require student engagement had been more difficult than they had first imagined. The available texts and other instructional materials didn't always fill the job. The local regional assistance center had recently developed a series of webinars that accompanied a clearinghouse of mathematics lessons. The LC complemented these webinars with their own collaborative discussion focused on what they learned, how it could be applied to their work, and any revisions or refinements they would make on the lessons provided to match their students' needs.

Step 6: Monitor and Refine Implementation

Just as educators have developed formative assessments of student learning in order to monitor progress toward an ultimate learning outcome, formative assessments are also needed to monitor the growth and use of new instructional and curricular classroom practices by teachers. Classroom observations, instructional rounds, and walk-throughs are useful ways to collect and monitor implementation.

A tool that measures the quality of implementation, which was introduced earlier in these steps, is the innovation configuration (IC) map. An IC map resembles a rubric with a continuum of practices that describe ideal implementation to not-yet-begun behaviors. It defines new practices *in operation*—describing what the teacher would do—almost like watching a video clip, only in words instead of pictures (Hall & Hord, 2011). This tool is invaluable when defining the desired change, monitoring development, and evaluating results.

An innovation configuration map can serve as an observation tool to monitor the progress of educators' use of new strategies. It can also serve as a self-assessment tool for educators to monitor their own progress. The monitoring data are used to determine next steps for individuals or groups of teachers, to differentiate professional learning or coaching, or to refine or revise current professional learning strategies. The purpose of monitoring is to support educators, providing assistance for continued growth or refinement of practices.

An example can be found in a well-established, long-term LC. They used an innovation configuration map to collect formative, monitoring data that showed that while some learning community members were making rapid progress toward the use of new classroom practices, others were not. The LC reviewed and discussed that data to determine actions to address that outcome. Their analysis discovered that team members who were making the most progress had already been introduced to the new practices 2 years earlier, felt more comfortable, and saw the connection between the strategies and student needs. As a result, the learning team created partnerships—one experienced member with another who has less experience—and asked them to plan together, observe and debrief lessons, and reflect on the new practice. Some partners even decided to coplan and coteach for additional support. This professional learning strategy is an appropriate response to the analysis of monitoring data. It also requires a high level of trust among LC members so that the focus is on supporting each other to learn new strategies rather than comparing differences.

A second issue to consider in Step 6 is the need for high-fidelity implementation of new practices. Have you heard of a program that was wildly successful in a neighboring district, but when brought to a new district, it did not fulfill its promise of higher scores and better test results? Those who have studied implementation of new practices and programs report one clear finding: High-quality implementation by a majority of staff members is required to make the highest gains in student results (Reeves, 2010). Reeves (2010) found a 13% improvement when high-fidelity practice was achieved. High-fidelity implementation of new strategies, therefore, becomes a component of educators' learning goals.

High-fidelity implementation of new practices requires identifying and focusing on the critical components identified in research (Marzano, Pickering, & Pollock, 2001). Some aspects of a new instructional practice are critical; others are nice but not necessary. For example, high-fidelity use of higher-order questioning, an aspect of the Common Core, involves developing appropriate questions, determining the appropriate time to ask questions, providing think and wait time for student reflecting, and scaffolding learning so that students are ready and skilled at answering higher-order questions, not just asking higher-order questions. High-fidelity use of student cooperative learning strategies involves teachers specifically developing students' collaborative skills so that they can work together more effectively and efficiently and not merely using interesting strategies to form heterogeneous teams.

In Step 6, an effective learning community will

- identify and define high-quality use of new classroom practices
- monitor the level of quality of implementation by colleagues
- use monitoring data to refine classroom practice
- support each other's continued refinement of new strategies and practices

---

More information about this step can be found in the Implementation and Data volumes within this series.

This Step in Action: The leadership team, Kristin, and the math LC were encouraged by their progress. The support they received from each other, Mary, and Clayton helped them accomplish much more than they expected.

Kristin felt the LC members were ready for the next challenge: to determine whether they were using the strategies with high quality or high fidelity. They all agreed that the curriculum adjustments were much harder to accomplish compared to using active engagement strategies during instruction. Kristin and Mary introduced the concept of high-fidelity practice and asked each member of the community to rate her- or himself on the ability to create lessons that encouraged, supported, and required student engagement. The team felt they were ready to have an outside assessment of their skills related to developing appropriate instructional materials.

Kristin and Mary contacted the regional assistance center, where staff had already planned to facilitate instructional rounds in local districts. They had begun to identify experts from local schools, districts, and universities who knew the Common Core and had experience with structuring active student engagement. The center staff had developed a set of criteria, formatted as an innovation configuration map, to determine the quality of implementation of these new practices. Kristin and Mary asked for a copy of the criteria to share with the team and identified dates when the rounds could be conducted.

The community reviewed the criteria and confirmed the date for the event. As the day approached, team members were becoming nervous. They felt they had made some huge gains in using active engagement strategies and reconfiguration lesson materials—but they weren't really sure.

The day arrived, data were collected, and feedback was provided. In a structured debriefing of the experience, each team member identified individual strengths and areas of growth. Kristin and Joe were very proud of the community and their willingness to have their work scrutinized by outside experts. They brought in a cake decorated with fresh fruit and a couple of bottles of sparkling apple juice to celebrate the event and mark the community's growth and accomplishments. Later, each teacher was asked to identify next steps to improve, refine, or perfect her or his new knowledge and skills.

Step 7: Evaluate Results

Finally, learning communities need to collect data and other evidence to determine whether their goal has been attained. Referring to their revised SMART goal is the first step. What did the team decide they would accomplish? What data or evidence was identified within the SMART goal for both students and teachers?

For example, let's use a SMART goal for educators that focuses on teachers' consistent, high-quality use of specific instructional strategies as measured by an IC map. The LC had already collected, with the assistance of the school's instructional coach, formative data concerning implementation of these strategies using an IC map. They decided to conduct another round of observations and also requested that each team member complete the same IC map as a self-assessment. The data revealed that community members had made progress over the course of the year, but all had not yet reached high-fidelity use of the new strategies. The LC decided to continue their focus on the instructional strategies for another quarter and again collect observational data. They also decided to make further changes to the way they were supporting each other's use of these new practices.

The LC also examines student learning results identified in the SMART goal. They analyze assessment results to identify strengths, successes, and needs. LC members identify any trends or patterns within the results that could help them create more refined goals in the next round of goal setting. The team also tries to make connections between their professional learning and student results. Did the classroom with higher-quality implementation make more gains? Did struggling students make higher gains when new instructional strategies were used? Making the connection between educator learning and student learning helps to reinforce the idea that teacher efforts and hard work impact student learning.

A purposeful reflection on what they learned throughout the cycle is important. Community members might reflect on questions such as the following:

- What did educators learn about their students and their own learning preferences and needs?
- Were there unexpected outcomes?
- What did they learn, individually or collectively, about the process of change?
- What did they learn about the success or failure of specific professional learning designs and strategies?
- What did they learn about how students reacted to new classroom strategies?
- What did LC members consider successful and what strategies would they change?

The final step in the cycle of continuous improvement moves naturally into beginning another round. Based on results and their reflection, they begin the cycle again by examining the data and determining how to continue to grow, learn from each other, and continue to support each other's progress.

> In Step 7, an effective learning community will
>
> - collect and analyze data identified in educator and student SMART goals
> - identify strengths, progress, needs, and next steps related to their goal
> - reflect on their experience and identify positives, negatives, successes, and failures
> - continue with a new round of the cycle

A more in-depth description of strategies can be found in the Data volume within this series.

This Step in Action: The math community was ready for its next challenge: to determine whether their work over the past months would accomplish their goal of improved student learning in their focus area. Their first opportunity was to examine the results of the district interim assessment. This assessment especially focused on their area of need— functions and algebraic thinking. Most of the time, they were not very excited about administering the assessment or looking forward to the results. This time they had a personal interest in the results. The community decided to review and analyze the results together. They did an item analysis for questions related to their goal area as well as all scores for the grade level to identify gains, trends, or lack of growth. The results were not dramatic but did show a trend toward closing the achievement gap. These trends were stronger in their area of focus, which encouraged them and made them feel their efforts paid off.

Mary brought a structured debriefing protocol that asked LC members to identify important events that occurred over the course of the year, how they felt about their LC work, what they learned from the process, and how their learning and working together could be used to accomplish future learning goals—what worked, what would they change, and what might they jettison. Their principal and

Resource C (page 91) is a self-assessment of the cycle of continuous improvement that the whole faculty, school leadership team, or individual learning communities can use to determine areas they might need to learn more about. Individuals should complete the self-assessment alone, then compile and average the results for each step in the cycle. Next, analyze the results to determine strengths and areas of need or improvement.

assistant principal sat in and participated in the debriefing, for they also had learned a lot about LCs.

They reflected on what they might do to prepare students for the state assessment given what they had learned, but also reflected on how to continue their work into the next year. The community did want to wait until the state assessment results were released before getting into next year's plans. After all, one of the things they had learned is that assessment results are the beginning and end of the cycle.

CONCLUSION

The purpose of our schools is the successful learning of all students. The most significant factor for achieving student success is the quality of teaching they receive in the school. This quality is maintained, increased, or enhanced through the continuous learning of the teaching staff and the administrators who support them. Where can this educator learning most profitably be conducted? The most powerful structure/strategy/setting for this activity is the community of professional learners.

Many allege that the simple convening of groups, or communities of educators such as grade-level teams in the elementary schools or academic department staff in secondary schools—perhaps even the whole school—constitutes the learning community. This is a gross misrepresentation of the learning community, for the learning community's purpose is the ongoing learning of the school staff, learning that is aligned with the learning needs of students, requiring complex actions of the educators who serve their students.

A major part of any school or school district's mission is to maintain a system of improving its work. Thus, almost every school district has a process for doing this that is grounded in the premise that

improvement is based on

changing practices that are not working well, for those that hold the potential for success, and that

learning what the new practice is and how to use it is imperative.

This requirement for deep learning of the "new way" fits the purpose of the learning community. It makes abundant good sense that the standards for professional learning should specify the learning community setting and its agenda as its first standard. It is here that attention is given to a system, process, or program of improvement undertaken by the learning community. This process for the first of the standards for professional learning is the steps of the cycle of continuous improvement and has been given major attention in this chapter's discussion.

But exercising these steps is done in the effective learning community when it operates as a self-organizing community, behaving in alignment with the research-based attributes of such a community. These six attributes have also been the focus of attention in this discussion of the first of the standards. In order for a group of educators to operate as an LC, there is much they must learn in order to become this powerful entity. Gaining expertise in using different conversation modes that fit the purpose of the conversation is an early skill to be developed (Garmston & Wellman, 2000). Developing interdependent thinking is vital as a basis for the community's collaborative interactions (see Sommers & Hord, 2013, and Roy, 2013).

As classroom-based educators form an LC, there are substantial actions required of the school's administrators/school leadership team. This team can support the learning community in significant ways, beginning with a time and regular schedule for meeting to engage in collaborative learning and work. Space, in some schools, can be a challenge and can be solved by administrative action. A significant responsibility to be acknowledged and addressed by the school's leadership team is the provision of material and human resources to support the growth of the community and its productive interactions. One such recently published resource is Donohoo's (2013) *Collaborative Inquiry for Educators* that presents a four-step process, including protocols, that groups use to engage in successful collaborative discussion, remembering that the LC, as noted by Lieberman and Miller in Chapter 1 of this volume, currently must operate in a "bureaucratic culture" as opposed to the "professional culture" dictated by the members' beliefs, values, and aspirations.

Thus, the learning community develops the knowledge, skills, and dispositions of *how* to act as a community of learners and *what* the community's work is. That is the goal of this chapter and the essence of implementing or developing and applying the learning communities standard. When the community operates in the manner suggested by the *how* and *what* described in this chapter, there is the strong likelihood that the community will develop collective responsibility for its students. Further, when "Learning Communities align their goals with those of the school and school system, engage in continuous professional learning, and hold all members collectively accountable for results," they will have achieved the outcomes of learning communities promoted by Learning Forward (Learning Forward, 2011, pp. 25–26).

Research has shown that the introduction of any new practice will require significant time for the new practice to be given attention and action for implementation, or installing it into the everyday practices of the classroom. For example, a reasonably simple academic curriculum will require 3 to 5 years for its high-quality implementation. The cycle of continuous improvement accompanied by the development of an effectively functioning learning community deserves no less, although in the setting of smaller groups of individuals, such as a grade-level learning community, new practices could be mastered much more efficiently. In this case support and facilitation for the implementation of new practices are part of the expectations of the learning community, as members coach and facilitate their colleagues' new practice. Doing so reduces impatience and frustration as new behaviors and tasks are learned.

It should be noted that while implementing the learning community standard is of significant importance, this standard should not operate as the only standard when designing professional learning for educators. There are an additional six standards that should be considered in providing professional learning. This means that the learning community is not a solo factor; the additional six standards should be given explicit attention, and each of these are the focus of attention in the other volumes in this series.

The development of learning communities is meant to increase higher-quality teaching by their educators and more successful learning for students—goals that we can all readily support and promote.

REFERENCES

Donohoo, J. (2013). *Collaborative inquiry for educators: A facilitator's guide to school improvement.* Thousand Oaks, CA: Corwin.

Gallimore, R., & Ermeling, B. A. (2010, April 14). Five keys to effective teacher learning teams. *Education Week, 29,* 29. Retrieved from www .edweek.org/ew/articles/2010/04/13/29gallimore.h29.html

Garmston, R., & Wellman, B. (2000). *The adaptive school: Developing and facilitating collaborative groups.* El Dorado Hills, CA: Four Hats Seminar.

Hall, G., & Hord, S. (2011). *Implementing change: Patterns, principles, and potholes* (3rd ed.). Boston: Allyn and Bacon.

Hirsh, S., & Hord, S. (2008). Leader and learner. *Principal Leadership, 9*(4), 26–30.

Hord, S. M., & Hirsh, S. A. (2009). The principal's role in supporting learning communities. *Educational Leadership, 66*(5), 22–23.

Hord, S. M., & Tobia, E. F. (2012). *Reclaiming our teaching profession: The power of educators learning in community.* New York: Teachers College Press.

Johnson, D., & Johnson, F. (2011). *Joining together: Group theory and group skills* (11th ed.). Upper Saddle River, NJ: Pearson.

Joyce, B., & Calhoun, E. (2010). *Models of professional development: A celebration of educators.* Thousand Oaks, CA: Corwin and NSDC.

Killion, J. (2008). *Assessing impact: Evaluating staff development* (2nd ed.). Thousand Oaks, CA: Corwin and NSDC.

Killion, J. (2011). Classroom visit. *Journal of Staff Development, 32*(2), 54–57.

Learning Forward. (2011). *Standards for professional learning.* Oxford, OH: Author. www.learningforward.org/standards.

Lock, K. (2006). Dear colleague, please come for a visit. *Teachers Teaching Teachers, 2*(2), 1–6.

Marzano, R., Pickering, D., & Pollock, J. (2001). *Classroom instruction that works.* Alexandria, VA: ASCD and McREL.

McDonald, J., Mohr, N., Dichter, A., & McDonald, E. (2007). *The power of protocols: An educator's guide to better practice* (2nd ed.). New York: Teachers College Press.

McTighe, J., & Emberger, M. (2006). Teamwork on assessments creates powerful professional learning. *Journal of Staff Development, 27*(1), 38–44.

Pfeffer, J., & Sutton, R. (2000). *The knowing-doing gap: How smart companies turn knowledge into action.* Cambridge, MA: Harvard Business School Press.

Reeves, D. (2010). *Transforming professional development into student results.* Alexandria, VA: ASCD.

Richardson, J. (2001). Group wise: Strategies for examining student work together. *Tools for Schools, 4*(4), 1–3. www.learningforward.org/docs/tools-for-learning-schools/tools2–01.pdf.

Richardson, J. (2004, February/March). Lesson study: Teachers learn how to improve instruction. *Tools for Schools*, pp. 1–7.

Roy, P. (2013). We instead of me: The teacher's role in engendering interdependent student thinking. In A. Costa and P. O'Leary (Eds.), *The power of the social brain* (pp. 129–139). New York: Teachers College Press.

Sommers, W., & Hord, S. (2013). Creating interdependent thinking among the school staff. In A. Costa and P. O'Leary (Eds.), *The power of the social brain* (69–74). New York: Teachers College Press.

Tobia, E. F., & Hord, S. M. (2012). I am a professional. *Journal of Staff Development, 33*(3), 16–20, 26.

Vescio, V., Ross, D., & Adams, A. (2008). A review of research on the impact of professional learning communities on teaching practice and student learning. *Teaching and Teacher Education, 24,* 80–91.

CHAPTER THREE

The Case Study

Valerie von Frank

When Superintendent Tom Trigg states Blue Valley School District's motto, "education beyond expectations," he has something to back up those three words.

He has a solid, 5-year strategic plan, a decade of continually improving student achievement data in the district, and a new target—to be not just the best midsized school system in the Kansas City metropolitan area or the Midwest, or even in the nation. In 2013, Blue Valley set out to outperform Finland, one of the world's highest-achieving nations, in math, reading, and science on the Programme for International Student Assessment (PISA) exam and created a social media campaign to #beatfinland. That's the short-term goal.

Blue Valley's long-term goal: to be the best in the world. Or, as the board of education states, *"Blue Valley Schools will create and implement a system that will result in our students being among the world's leaders in academic achievement."* Achieving that goal may not be far in the future. Blue Valley, a suburban district just outside of the state's third-largest city, has a recent history of high achievement.

- While Blue Valley consistently scores higher than the rest of the United States, students' scores in math and reading on the Programme for International Student Assessment exam place Blue Valley seventh and fourth in the world respectively, according to the district's review.

- It is the only district in the country with more than 20,000 students to have achieved Adequate Yearly Progress as defined in the No Child Left Behind Act in every school, grade level, and subgroup over 10 consecutive years, according to a study from the University of Missouri, Kansas City.
- In 2012, 97.5% of the district's students scored proficient or above on reading and 97% scored proficient or above on math on the Kansas State Assessment.
- More impressively, 55% of the system's students scored in the state's top, exemplary category in reading, and 54.5% were exemplary in math in 2012. In 2002, just 21.0% scored in the top band in reading and 29.9% in the top band in math.
- The district had 43 National Merit finalists in 2012.
- All five of Blue Valley's high schools were on *Newsweek*'s list of top schools in the nation in 2012 and again in 2013.
- All five high schools are on the *Washington Post*'s most challenging high schools list in 2013.

"We've had to start looking not just at national comparisons now, but at where we line up internationally and to benchmark against the top schools internationally," Trigg said. "If we don't, then we have the potential to become stagnant. We have to keep raising the bar for our leadership team, our teachers, our kids."

> Blue Valley School District is located in Overland Park, Kansas, outside of Kansas City, and covers approximately 91 square miles. With more than 20,000 students in grades K–12, the district has 34 schools, including five high schools (Grades 9–12), nine middle schools (Grades 6–8) and 20 elementary schools (Grades K–5).
>
> Its student population is 79% white, 10% Asian/Pacific Islander, 5% Hispanic, 3% African American, 4% other.

The suburban district community is largely white, educated, and middle class. Trigg acknowledges that some educators might say he has the deck stacked in his favor based on his district's demographics. He responds that public schools don't choose the students they have, and educators are responsible for showing a continual upward trend in student growth and achievement with whatever students they have.

For Blue Valley, that has meant making sure every child is proficient, including subgroups such as special education students, those from homes in lower socioeconomic brackets, and those whose first language is not English. Beyond that, it's meant continually increasing the number of students not just meeting or exceeding expectations on the state assessment but moving into the top category of exemplary.

The district has produced a video it's dubbed the "dancing dots" that plots math and reading scores on the state assessment on a grid from 2000 onward and shows the progression from a scattering of dots in the early years of around 60% and clustering at 80% then moving rapidly after 2008 for all schools to 95% or higher for both math and reading at every school and remaining at those levels.

The upward trend also has meant maintaining composite ACT scores of nearly 25 even as the number of students taking the exam increased 1.5 times over a decade. And it's meant tripling the number of AP exams students have taken while still having 82% score 3 or above.

Trigg said the district began to improve when it put in place a strategic plan, focused on its mission, and structured ongoing staff development in professional learning communities (PLCs).

STRATEGIC PLANNING

When Trigg became superintendent in 2005, he fine-tuned the strategic plan, holding a town hall meeting to get community input on what district priorities should be. The strategic plan creates targets that leaders can use to set specific, measurable goals that they then review annually and report progress on publicly.

The district's 2010 through 2015 strategic plan includes seven succinct performance targets:

Performance Target 1: All schools and all grade levels will achieve the Standard of Excellence on the Kansas State Assessments. On each state assessment, special focus will continue to be placed on the performance of identifiable subgroups as well as the percentage of students scoring at the exemplary level.

Performance Target 2: K–8 students will participate in Measures of Academic Progress (MAP) testing in order to provide diagnostic and progress data.

Performance Target 3: Schools will show yearly increases in the percentage of students who meet college readiness benchmarks on the ACT.

Performance Target 4: Schools will show annual increases in the number of students enrolled in college-credit-bearing courses.

Performance Target 5: Students will be provided with the experiences and opportunities to be "ready" for college and career.

Performance Target 6: Students will be provided with the experiences and opportunities to enhance their responsibilities in their community and in the world at large.

Performance Target 7: All students will have access to curriculum-embedded technological tools, will demonstrate knowledge of the appropriate use of such tools, and will be able to apply their use in a variety of contexts.

As part of the strategic plan, leaders developed a districtwide system of intervention for when students weren't learning and gave teachers time to collaborate and learn together to improve their instruction so they could better help students. Trigg said the central office needed to determine what materials and curriculum would be used across the system and purchase those, relieving principals of that burden and ensuring consistency, and then allowed principals to work with their staffs as instructional leaders at the building level on supporting teachers in learning best practices.

Blue Valley High School's principal at the time, Dennis King, already had started learning communities at his school. The district adopted the practice systemwide, making it a goal that every teacher in the district would have time to collaborate in grade-level or content-area teams based on the district's priorities.

"You pull people together and let them collaborate," Trigg said, "and all of a sudden they're helping one another ensure the success of these interventions and you have a systemwide effort."

The district worked with the teachers' association to create time for teachers during the workday. Elementary school grade-level teams use their planning period each week for grade-level meetings or time during special subjects—art, music, physical education, or foreign language—for grade-level meetings. They generally have about 30 minutes at a time to meet, depending on the day. They often voluntarily add time, meeting before or after school or over lunch. In addition, all schools use early-release days as time for professional learning.

At the secondary level, middle school teachers have double planning periods daily and each school has flexibility in choosing how to structure that PLC time by grade, content area, or whole-staff professional learning on common needs, such as an issue around special education or data collection. High schools have a later start each Thursday, when students are scheduled for academic classes a half hour later, although they still are allowed in the buildings for computer or library time. The high school teams then have 50 minutes a week, plus an additional half hour every other Tuesday. They are charged with unit planning, lesson planning, looking at student data, creating common assessments, analyzing where students are achieving, and working together to determine how to improve instruction so that student learning improves.

The district also has brought school staffs together routinely in job-alike teams. The cross-school collaborations are particularly beneficial for singleton teachers such as art teachers.

Trigg said developing a collaborative spirit among buildings was an important objective. Learning and collaboration are modeled throughout the central office and the system as simply the way Blue Valley does business.

"We had to develop the idea that for our system to excel, it was not enough for one or two buildings to do well," Trigg said. "A true PLC is systemic, not just teacher to teacher and not just teachers and a principal in a building. It's cross-district. It's principal to principal. It's a principal sharing their best practices with another principal. It's absolutely all for one and one for all. It's a buy-in to the district and system as a whole, knowing that if we get the whole system to excel, then every building is going to have a place in that."

He said he constantly reinforces the message with community and staff that the district's mission is unprecedented academic success and unparalleled personal growth for every student. And, he says, that mission is accomplished through professional learning communities.

"PLCs are not just a time to meet but are a way to operate," Trigg said. "A PLC is a PLC 24 hours a day, not just when teachers are together at an assigned time. It's people collaborating, analyzing data, sharing work together constantly, consistently. PLCs are dynamic."

Trigg said the culture in the district, like student achievement, continues to improve, but leaders are not resting.

"The minute you think you've arrived, you're in trouble," he said. "If you develop any kind of hubris, you are setting yourself up for failure. The leadership team has to always be on the lookout and always setting higher goals."

⋘⋙

For Principal Scott Bacon, the hardest fact he had to face in 2013 was that Blue Valley High School had missed the mark. One junior had not met state standards in reading, giving the school a success rate of 99.7%. In math, 97.6% of students met or exceeded the state's standards. It was close but not enough.

"We have a vision of what we want to become," Bacon said. His school had set out a dozen years earlier to achieve 100%, each student proficient in each subject, no matter what.

Bacon's frustration was evident as he explained that the one junior not meeting the reading standard was a foreign exchange student whose first language is not English. The school has made a concerted effort around different subgroups, particularly focusing on special education students.

The main subgroup in the student population is special education students, and so special educators and general educators have developed partnerships, Bacon said, that have enabled the special education students to succeed. When two students were one point away from meeting proficiency in reading, teachers decided to provide small-group and individualized instruction to help them raise the bar. Special education teachers coteach, and teachers have been trained in specific strategies and curricular approaches to meet students' specialized needs. Teachers also engage students in tracking their own learning.

Bacon talked about the school's sense of mission as he reflected on a decade's worth of data that show continual improvement and vowed a renewed effort to meet the goal. Phrases with the same theme cropped up throughout his speech: "Collaboration is an expectation;" "Teamwork makes the dream work."

For Blue Valley, the pathway to all improvements is through professional learning communities. Change only comes about when teachers have time to gather, analyze their instruction, and together discuss what different approach to take.

"We want to be a high-performing professional learning community," Bacon said. "If we are able to answer the four questions plus one every day, students will continue to grow and perform at the highest levels. We have strategies and practices that answer those questions, and we're very clear what those are."

The four questions are the school's PLC frame: What do we want students to learn? How do we know if they have learned it? What do we do to help them learn it? How will we motivate students to learn? The "plus one," Bacon said, focuses on developing positive relationships with and among students.

Bacon works hard to develop the school culture, beginning with modeling learning communities through the leadership team, which is its own learning community. The leadership team, comprising the principal, assistant principal of curriculum and instruction, seven department heads, and the district school-improvement specialist, meets weekly to collaborate and discuss issues such as decreasing the percentage of students earning Ds and Fs. They participate in book studies often centering on leadership, such as Daniel Pink's *Drive*. Department chairs then carry that learning back to their own teams.

The learning communities begin their work before students return to school in August. Staff have 4 days of professional development each year before classes resume. On the first day, after Bacon's welcoming remarks and tone setting for the year, departments spend two and a half hours in their own learning communities. It's a time to review group norms, go over data, and work as a group to set a department SMART goal.

"There's accountability," Bacon said. "We want to make sure that we are measuring up to what we want to be, and if not, that we ask what we can do about it."

Bacon shares a timeline with the PLCs at the beginning of the year that sets up the expectations for the groups for the year. The top of the document states a rationale for learning communities: The purpose of professional learning communities is to engage all staff in a *systematic* process in which we work *interdependently* to *analyze* and *impact* professional practice in order to *improve* student and staff learning.

He outlines five specific purposes for the use of the PLC time to staff in the formal timeline document:

- Develop and/or revise learning targets and common formative and summative assessments
- Analyze and interpret data as they relate to instruction, assessment, and classroom interventions
- Share and develop best-practice instructional strategies
- Collaboratively revise curriculum maps
- Periodically reflect on practice and procedures

The document then lists each of the four key PLC questions, under which are specific strategies and expectations for PLCs, as well as indicators of how the principal expects to know whether the target is being met.

"Every behavior that we expect of the PLC has an identified product and a completion date that is clear up front," Bacon said.

For example, one item under the third question, "What do we do to help them learn it?" is the expectation that learning communities will "embed WICR strategies (writing, inquiry, collaboration, reading) into the instruction/learning experiences." Teachers are expected to use strategies such as Cornell notes, writing-to-learn, Costa's and Bloom's levels of questioning, Socratic seminars, think-pair-share, jigsaw, team games and tournaments, peer editing, Kagan structures, reading for purpose, frontloaded vocabulary, text structure, annotation skills, and graphic organizers. On the outline, Bacon states that he will see the evidence of these in walk-throughs and in samples that teachers provide in portfolios.

Each PLC then gives Bacon a copy of the learning teams' vision, SMART goal(s), team norms, method of consensus, and classroom and departmental interventions. Bacon publishes all of the learning communities' SMART goals in a booklet that is distributed to each staff member so that everyone in the building can see what others are doing.

"It shows everybody that all are being asked to do the same thing," Bacon said.

At the end of each quarter, every department answers reflection questions. They review assessment data, look at how close they are to their SMART goals, and consider their instruction and how it has improved. Teachers rate their work on areas pertaining to each of the core questions around learning communities. They use a Likert scale, and Bacon defines each rating as follows:

1—We have not yet completed this work.

2—Our work is in the discussion and/or developing stages.

3—Our work is developed but is undergoing revision.

4—Our work is thoroughly developed, frequently revisited with little revision needed.

5—Our work is thoroughly developed and could be used as a model for others.

For example, under the question "What is it that we want students to learn?" is this statement: A curriculum map/pacing guide has been developed to monitor the effective delivery of learning targets, instruction, and assessment.

Members of the learning community provide a rating in three areas:

- A curriculum map/pacing guide has been developed for each unit of instruction.
- The curriculum map/pacing guide includes assessments and instructional activities that align with the learning targets.
- Notes and comments arc included in the curriculum map/ pacing guide that refer to the effectiveness of the implementation and administration of activities and assessments.

"It starts at the beginning in terms of learning," Bacon said. "We ask every PLC to be very clear about each unit and what they expect students to learn—the learning targets. Not only should the teachers know, but they should articulate that to the students. The expectation is that PLCs will develop common learning targets for units."

Bacon looks for those targets as he visits classrooms and observes lessons, asking students what they are learning and the purpose of the day's lesson. The learning communities are expected to develop common quarterly assessments and determine whether and when those need to be revised.

When a department wants to create a common assessment and teachers need time to work together on it, Bacon arranges for substitutes for a half day to allow them to collaborate.

"To move student learning forward, it can't be one person at a time," Bacon said. "When we show our data to new teachers, their mouths drop open. In this building, you need to get on board. It's OK to say you don't know. There are three others teaching what you're teaching who will brainstorm with you. First and foremost, we have a collaborative, collegial family environment.

"Our teachers have been sharing instructional ideas and strategies with a high level of credibility for 15 years," he continued. "It's pretty exciting when you see your performance continue to grow. Still, it's always a work in progress. There's always room for improvement."

ॐॐ

Every Thursday, from 7:30 a.m. to 8:55 a.m., the teachers at Blue Valley High School gather for "sacred time." That's what the principal calls it. It's what the teachers call it. Central administrators refer to PLC time this way, too. It is the teachers' professional time together, one of the cornerstone commitments in the system's strategic plan. (See box.)

Jason Peres, who has taught for more than a decade at Blue Valley High School, is in his third year as department chair. He has never

---

BLUE VALLEY SCHOOL DISTRICT'S STRATEGIC PLAN COMMITMENTS

- We will make a continuous effort to reallocate resources, adopt innovative programs, and critically evaluate current practices to ensure academic excellence.

- **We are committed to Professional Learning Communities as the means of continuous school improvement.**

- We are committed to maintaining and improving an efficiently operated organization and will benchmark the district against peer school districts and other entities in key operational areas to ensure this commitment.

- We are committed to maintaining an environment whereby patrons are increasingly engaged and satisfied with the quality of Blue Valley Schools, and will measure this engagement and satisfaction on a regular basis.

Source: Blue Valley Strategic Plan, 2010–2015; emphasis added

taught without the benefit of a professional learning community and so, when a teacher new to the school and department approached him for advice, he naturally offered his course materials as well as his strategies and tips for teaching it.

"She said, 'Do you mind if I use this?' I said, 'Of course, that's why we're here,'" he said. "Where she was from, everybody was an independent contractor and nobody shared their materials because secretly they all wanted to be the best and they all were trying to monopolize the best strategies. They wanted to look great to the kids so the kids would want to take *their* courses.

"Here," he continued, "we want our *department* to be the best, and we want to make a difference."

To make that difference, Peres takes what he has learned in the high school leadership learning community studies about motivation and his research on the collective intelligence of teams and applies it to leading the department PLC. He works to ensure that each of the 12 teachers in the room has a voice, a challenge in what he calls "probably the most philosophical group in the school," but a necessity.

So at the end of each school year, Peres surveys his department staff on their professional learning needs, asks them what areas they want to pursue the following year, requests comments about the PLC, and then uses the data over the summer to outline a plan. When the group first gets together, he presents the summary to them at the welcome meeting, reviews the past year, discusses themes, and asks for feedback.

"Teaching is a science experiment," he said. "We try something, share with the group what we attempt to do. If it doesn't work, we share that. If it works, we share it. And that way everybody gets better."

Even before the teachers were asked to integrate Common Core State Standards, the social studies PLC had worked over 2 years planning four strands that would run throughout the curriculum to foster key skill sets for students, such as purposeful writing and communication. With that planning completed and the teachers' survey data about their professional learning needs, Peres began the 2013 through 2014 school year PLC meeting with two goals: to create a rubric that would allow teachers to have every senior write a research paper and to discuss how to handle late assignments.

Teachers in the PLC had discussed the idea of requiring every senior to write a research paper but were concerned about having time to grade them. After working on the core skill sets as a group, they brainstormed a solution: Bring all the papers to the PLC and work as a team to review the papers.

"Now we're creating the rubric, and everyone in the department owns it," Peres said. "Everybody grades 15 papers. We get immediate data and have immediate discussion of how kids are learning, what are their strengths, what are their weaknesses. Then teachers can take that back and make changes to their instruction in the classroom. Those are things we decided as a department to do."

Peres said each whole-department PLC begins with a few minutes to share.

"Someone will say, 'I'm doing this grading practice. What do you know that works well?'" Peres said. Teachers share solutions. Sometimes, they offer guidance. "It's not always rainbows," he said. "Sometimes it's, 'I've got this really challenging kid. This is how they responded to me. I really got into it with them. What do you guys think? How should I handle them? What should I do to make it better?'"

Often, then, a teacher will lead the group in a specific area of expertise. For example, two teachers who teach Advanced Placement government presented information about writing expectations and a rubric at the beginning of the year to lay the groundwork for the group's creation of its own rubric for the senior research papers.

The social studies department works in a learning community as a whole every other week, allowing course-alike teachers to work together to share more content-specific planning in alternate weeks. Each department within the school decides for itself how best to allocate the time and how best to use it.

Adam Wade, who heads the math department, said math teachers spend each Thursday morning in small groups that they join for the year focusing on two different classes. A teacher may work in a small group with one or two others who teach Algebra I and geometry, for example. The content-alike groups meet for about a half hour each.

It's a challenge to get teachers not to use those small groups for planning lessons, Wade said. He said he wants teachers to use that time to make sure common assessments are viable, for example to answer questions such as: Does this quiz measure what we want it to measure? Does it have an appropriate number of questions and the right questions?

Or teachers could use that time to discuss formative assessments they might use with students throughout a unit after an introductory lesson, such as warm-up problems for factoring, and decide how to collect and use student performance data.

"What insights can we gain?" Wade said. "My students did terrible on this particular portion of the test. Yours did great? What did you do differently? Let's talk about that."

After the small-group work, the department spends time as a whole on a common issue, such as how a topic is being taught one year versus in the subsequent class to make sure that concepts are represented in the same way, he said, or aligning formative assessments.

Wade said the work can be "tricky at times" when teachers find areas in which a colleague may have outperformed them.

"That's one of the hardest things to attack—what did you do differently," he said. "It takes a lot to ask that. But the benefits outweigh the personal pride. If you were to ask every person in my department, I don't think they're viewing it as my students versus your students. We all need to be thinking of all of our students for all 4 years."

Wade remembers working as a student teacher in what the school called a professional learning community. It was nothing like his experience at Blue Valley.

"The department chair talked at us for half an hour," he said. "It was a meeting. There wasn't any learning going on. I didn't have anyone to talk to about how I was explaining something in my classes. I didn't have any idea of how other people's students were doing, how other people were teaching a concept. I didn't have any idea if my students were making the same mistakes or different mistakes than other people's, so realistically, how could I have expected to get any better? How could I expect my students to improve?

"We had no common assessments. I had no data to look at comparing how my students did on a topic versus someone else's. We just had no barometers. I thought what I was doing was fine, but how did I really know?"

The last decade at Blue Valley has changed that. And like Peres, Wade can hardly imagine a different way of working.

"When student learning is the number-one objective, why on earth would we not do this?" he asked. "I would not consider working at a school without PLCs. It's too big of a part now of how I teach and how I improve as a professional."

THE VIEW FROM THREE LEVELS

JASON PERES, Blue Valley High School social studies department chairperson

The PLC model is about getting creative with the schedule and creating time for teachers to make a difference. And the other thing is, the professional learning community itself has to establish a purpose and it has to have autonomy.

A lot of districts struggle with giving teachers autonomy because they think teachers won't do the work. I've found when you give people autonomy, they're more motivated to work and they'll produce a higher-quality product. You have to have some data to show students are learning. It can't all be anecdotal. But the teachers at Blue Valley feel they have autonomy in their PLC time to do what they think is going to make the difference for student learning. The accountability does not come from the principal looking over our shoulders. Through our PLC, we collaborate and hold each other accountable. We share so much that we immediately see the expectations, and there's pressure to do a good job because our peers see what we're doing.

Some schools think that PLC time is teachers sitting down and talking about who needs supplies—who needs pens and pencils and construction paper. That's not what PLCs are about. PLCs are about what we want kids to know, how we will know that kids are learning it, what we will do when they don't learn, and what we will do if they already know it. If you're talking about something in a PLC that doesn't address those four questions, you're probably off task.

My responsibility is to make sure our department is meeting the school goals and executing our own plan at the same time. We generate a purpose for our department in our PLC and we execute our own purpose, and then we share that out with the rest of the school so that we all get on the same page.

There's value in professionals sitting down and talking about what we see in our classrooms and our observations. When you have those conversations, you give teachers professional respect. That's the beauty of the professional learning community. We talk about learning and best strategies, and data are the measure.

If I don't have colleagues to bounce ideas off of, I just keep doing the same thing year after year. With professional learning communities, we have all these discussions about what it is we do.

᪣

DENNIS KING, former principal, Blue Valley High School

Our school had flatlined—we were not improving. So I asked the question, "Is this really the school that we want to be?" And as a staff, we looked at our data and said, "No, we aren't."

We had thought we were pretty good, but all we had to do was look at the data. We were at a spot where we thought we were good based upon previous years. The data showed we had a number of kids with Ds and Fs. We didn't have a lot of kids with high levels on Advanced Placement scores. Every piece of data indicated we had to do something. If not, we should expect the school to continue to perform the same way. And we had a lot of teachers who were prideful in the school; we had to point out that the way we were doing things wasn't good enough.

We began by tackling the culture. We talked about the school we would want to become and the collective commitments we'd have to have to get there. We had a high graduation rate and kids going to Ivy League schools, but we had a large number of kids who *weren't* learning at high levels. We had to look at that. Is it OK to have only 80% of kids moving on? And of the kids moving on, how many are moving on without taking remedial freshman math class in college?

At first, I rejected that our school was where it was. I had every excuse and reason that our school was different. Then when you sit down and look at the numbers, you see that really *is* us. I believe that when things are great, you keep asking what we can do to keep improving, and if you're not doing well, you look in the mirror.

At the time, we were the only school in the district doing PLCs, so I had to go to the district office to lobby for professional learning communities and explain the rationale. Then we had to get clear on what the work is.

We talked as a faculty about our mission. Then I created time within the day for teams to meet, and we went from there. We just got focused. Unless we have 100% of kids at high levels, we have a ways to grow. We built teachers' capacity and time for kids to get extra help. We stayed true to the process, and we saw dramatic changes right away.

〜〜〜

SUE DOLE, deputy superintendent of education services

You have to model professional learning communities within the district office staff. We are our own professional learning community. I have a staff comprising 14 executive directors and directors and we meet once a week to focus our conversation on learning.

(Continued)

(Continued)

We're currently reading *Cultures Built to Last: Systemic PLCs at Work*, by Richard DuFour and Michael Fullan. Our questions in our own professional learning community are always centered around, How does this apply to the work that we do? All of us supervise groups of people on projects, and we must continually ask ourselves, How is the work that *we* do affecting our buildings, how does it improve our district, how is it interrelated among groups of staff? Always we're looking at district staff as well as building-level staff. So the first piece is that we are modeling learning in PLCs.

Then we work in PLCs with our principals, within what we call family groups, and we try to model the work of PLCs, to be a PLC in action as well as a set of trainers working with principals. We provide development that extends their skill sets and information that they take back to their buildings to share with their faculties. Principals lead a portion of the professional development for their faculties based on their own faculties' needs as defined by their school learning plans, which is what we call the school improvement plan. The fact that principals take the foremost role as instructional leaders allows us to be very consistent in messaging across our whole district and allows us to really focus on those pieces of our district strategic plan that we consider to be most important. That message, learning, and modeling then filter down through building-level professional learning communities.

We in the central office often use an analogy from our director of professional development's grandfather, who was a farmer and a very wise man. He always said if you want a white fence post on your farm, you start by painting the fence post white. But you can't walk away and leave that post. You have to keep painting it. You also have to keep painting those things that are important in your life. One of the tools for painting the important things is PLCs.

Note: Quoted material from Scott Bacon, Sue Dole, Dennis King, Jason Peres, Tom Trigg, and Adam Wade is used with permission.

Resources

Resource A

WHAT ARE SMART GOALS?

The acronym SMART comes from the five components of SMART goals.

- Strategic and Specific
- Measurable
- Attainable
- Results-based
- Time-bound

Patricia Roy (2007) describes SMART goals this way:

Strategic goals focus on high-priority issues that are part of a comprehensive school or district plan. **Specific** goals focus on the precise needs of students for whom the goal is aimed.

For example, strategic goals are determined, in part, from analyzing student achievement and behavioral data. When this data is disaggregated, commonalities and differences among student groups become more apparent.

Measurable goals contain information about how a change will be calculated. The goal identifies the tool or instrument that will be used to measure whether the school or

> "Set priorities for your goals. A major part of successful living lies in the ability to put first things first. Indeed, the reason most major goals are not achieved is that we spend our time doing second things first."
>
> Robert J. McKain

team has attained the desired results. Measurement is best accomplished by using a number of different tools and strategies. If a consistent pattern of change is seen through multiple measures, then the school will have greater confidence that its actions made the difference. For example, teams would use results from state assessment data, national standardized assessments, district or school performance measures, discipline referrals, or other instruments that measure performance, outcomes, or results.

Attainable goals include actions that the school can control or influence and that can be accomplished with existing resources. The team setting the goal identifies a baseline or starting point when determining whether a goal is attainable. The team also needs to know how much time and what other resources are available to accomplish the goal. There is a delicate balance between setting a goal that is compelling and energizing to staff while not becoming so unrealistic that educators are discouraged from accepting the goal because they believe it's not possible to reach.

Results-based goals identify specific outcomes that are measurable or observable. Results could be expressed as attaining a certain level of student achievement in a content area, an increase in the number of students who improve in a certain area, or as improved performance as defined and measured by a performance rubric or clear criteria.

Many school people confuse "activity" with "results." They place into their school improvement goals the "means" they will use to accomplish the goal, such as implementing a new mathematics program or using cooperative learning strategies, rather than describing the outcome they expect for students. Results-based means a clear and specific description of the results of the school's activities.

Time-bound goals identify the amount of time required to accomplish it. Goals are sometimes more compelling when there is a sense of urgency attached to them. A pre-determined time frame can create a sense of urgency and make the goal a priority to staff and students.

In short, SMART goals help us determine which of our efforts is making a difference, encourage us to set benchmarks to monitor progress, and identify specific evaluation measures.

Strategic and specific   *Results-based*

                                Measurable

All district students will perform at the "meets or exceeds" expectations level on the state writing assessment by the 2010–11 school year.

Attainable: the school has three years
    to improve from 70% to 100%   *Time-bound*

Source: Roy, P. (2007). A *tool kit for quality professional development in Arkansas.* Oxford, OH: NSDC.

Resource B

Resource B Innovation Configuration Map for the Professional Learning Community

The PLC Member				
Component A: Shares the responsibility for leading the work of a professional learning community				
1	2	3	4	5
Seeks or accepts the role and responsibility for leading the work of a PLC; promotes the identification and assignment of potential leadership roles for PLC colleagues; develops insights and suggestions for creating leadership roles for others; shares possibilities for leadership equitably with other members of the PLC; participates in decision making based on sound judgment	Accepts, although initially tentative, a role and responsibility for guiding and supporting the PLC's work; shares insights and suggestions for creating leadership roles and promotes the assignment of potential roles for PLC colleagues; shares possibilities for leadership equitably with other PLC members	Assumes PLC leadership roles reluctantly; promotes assigning such roles to other PLC colleagues; begins to feel comfortable in playing a role in leading the PLC	Avoids taking leadership roles; lobbies consistently for the same colleagues to take roles in leading the PLC	Fails to consider self as a leader; gives little to no attention to this role and its value in the PLC
Evidence				

Component B: Expresses and shares a school vision focused on teacher and student learning			
1	2	3	4
Articulates own personal beliefs and values; discusses these with impunity and to gain consensus; uses the consensus to collegially formulate a vision for the school that relentlessly focuses on adult and student learning; provides energy and enthusiasm for sharing and promoting the vision to colleagues and to school and neighborhood communities	Shares his/her vision of the school's purpose; energetically promotes his/her vision, but collaborates to gain consensus for the school's vision that highlights educators' and students' continuous learning; plans with colleagues to promote the vision with parents	Supports the school's vision that focuses on student learning; maintains communication with parents that reports events and activities that enable the school to realize its vision	Forgets that the school has a vision; neglects to apply it personally and fails to share the vision with the school's constituency
Evidence			

Source: Reprinted by permission of the Publisher. From Shirley M. Hord and Edward F. Tobia, *Reclaiming Our Teaching Profession: The Power of Educators Learning in the Community.* New York: Teachers College Press. Copyright © 2012 by Teachers College, Columbia University. All rights reserved. www.tcpress.org

(Continued)

Resource B (Continued)

Component C: Engages in continuous intentional and collective learning				
1	2	3	4	5
Explores a wide variety of student data sources to identify areas of students' needs for improvement; establishes, with colleagues, a focus for change in teaching/learning practices that address students' needs; determines collaboratively what teachers will need to learn; decides collectively how teachers will do this learning; participates in the learning; plans with the PLC members how new practice will be implemented in classrooms and how student learning will be assessed; uses evidence of student learning to review, assess, and revise implementation activities and adjusts instruction based on that review	Uses multiple data sources to identify areas of students' low performance; determines a priority focus for change in instructional practice, targeting students' needs; delineates what teachers will need to learn related to the new practice and how they will do the learning; participates in the learning and planning to transfer new practice to classrooms	Uses a variety of multiple data sources to identify areas of students' low performance; specifies change(s) that will increase student performance; identifies the learning that teachers will need to accomplish; participates in the learning	Employs state achievement tests as the basis for determining action to take to address students' poor performance; works with PLC colleagues to plan and take action	Uses the PLC meeting time for planning with colleagues for materials and other resources for teaching the established units of study; discusses which resources to order, but no further conversation is devoted to instruction
Evidence				

Source: Reprinted by permission of the Publisher. From Shirley M. Hord and Edward F. Tobia, *Reclaiming Our Teaching Profession: The Power of Educators Learning in the Community.* New York: Teachers College Press. Copyright © 2012 by Teachers College, Columbia University. All rights reserved. www.tcpress.org

Component D: Provides, receives, and uses feedback on classroom teaching/learning practices				
1	2	3	4	5
Invites colleagues to observe specified teaching activity and to provide feedback that will be used to change and enhance practice; visits colleagues on invitation to observe and offer feedback; responds to hosting colleagues and visiting colleagues on the schedule and direction of the principal; shares expertise and instructional ideas with colleagues during PLC meetings, their lunch hour, planning time, and after school; reflects on his/her practices and related feedback and adjusts	Invites and schedules PLC colleagues to observe and provide feedback on a specific teaching activity; visits colleagues on invitation to observe and offer feedback for improvement; shares successful teaching activities informally during PLC meetings, at the lunch hour, during planning time, and after school	Serves as host and as visiting teacher, inviting colleagues to observe specific activities in order to share feedback; provides feedback when requested to others; shares expertise with other members	Shares lessons and classroom activities that students enjoyed	
Evidence				

Source: Reprinted by permission of the Publisher. From Shirley M. Hord and Edward F. Tobia, *Reclaiming Our Teaching Profession: The Power of Educators Learning in the Community.* New York: Teachers College Press. Copyright © 2012 by Teachers College, Columbia University. All rights reserved. www.tcpress.org

(Continued)

Resource B (Continued)

Component E: Uses structures and schedules to advance the PLC's work

1	2	3	4	5
Solicits the scheduling of a regular and frequent time for the PLC to meet; seeks a comfortable and available space for the PLC's regular meetings; articulates, with colleagues, norms that share expectations and guide the community's behaviors; appears on time and prepared for the PLC's meetings; uses the time and meeting space for engaging in the learning work of the PLC; encourages colleagues in their participation	Persuades administrators to find/create time for regular PLC meetings; surveys the staff to identify a location for the regular meetings of the PLC; arrives on time and prepared for engaging in the meeting's shared agenda	Implores administrators to identify the time for regular PLC meetings; pleads for a comfortable and regular location to be identified for the PLC meetings	Takes no action on behalf of the scheduling and other structures to make it possible to meet	
Evidence				

Component F: Participates in the development and application of relationship factors in support of the PLC's work				
1	2	3	4	5
Approaches the initial PLC meetings eagerly with an open (and receiving) mind and heart; articulates and endorses team/PLC learning in order to become more effective; promotes positive PLC relationships through both pleasant and productive interactions; exhibits trustworthiness through delivering on promises; demonstrates regard for colleagues and respect for their ideas and suggestions	Encourages colleagues enthusiastically regarding the initial meetings and endorses their potential for increased teacher effectiveness, student learning, and staff morale; increases positive PLC relationships through consistent pleasant and productive conversations and activity; delivers on promises and demonstrates trustworthiness; expresses regard for colleagues	Promotes colleagues' attendance and participation at meetings through persistent but pleasant reminders of the potential benefits and pleasurable interactions; shares pleasant conversations focused on adult and student learning to promote harmony; serves as a buffer when conversations veer unpleasantly; congratulates colleagues on both large and small "conquests"	Demonstrates pleasant interactions and exemplifies reliability, dependability, and transparency	
Evidence				

Source: Reprinted by permission of the Publisher. From Shirley M. Hord and Edward F. Tobia, *Reclaiming Our Teaching Profession: The Power of Educators Learning in the Community.* New York: Teachers College Press. Copyright © 2012 by Teachers College, Columbia University. All rights reserved. www.tcpress.org

Resource C

Resource C Survey: Use of the Cycle of Continuous Improvement

The whole faculty, school leadership team (SLT), or individual learning teams can conduct a self-assessment of their understanding and use of the cycle of continuous improvement. Each step in the cycle is provided along with essential elements. Individuals should indicate on the scale how well they use that component in their work in learning teams or to accomplish schoolwide goals. List any evidence to substantiate the ratings. The SLT could use this as a self-assessment of its work to accomplish schoolwide improvement goals.

Expert Use: Use with high frequency all of the component elements

Competent Use: Use with high frequency but only some of the component elements

Emerging Use: Use with sporadic frequency and only a few of the component elements

No Use: Have not used this element in their professional learning work

Elements	Expert Use	Competent Use	Emerging Use	No Use
The use of data to determine student and educator learning needs • Use student, teacher, and school data to determine needs • Staff participates in data analysis				
Identification of shared goals for student and educator learning • Goals are developed in cooperation with staff/group members so that they become mutual goals • Goals are based on data analysis				

Elements	Expert Use	Competent Use	Emerging Use	No Use
• Alignment between what students need to learn and what educators need to learn • Goals written in a SMART format				
Professional learning to extend educators' knowledge and skills • Content aligns with educator and student learning goal • Process includes collaboration among peers • Job-embedded strategies employed				
Selection and implementation of appropriate evidence-based strategies to achieve student and educator learning goals • Use of new strategies in the classroom • Strategies have evidence of impact on student and adult learning • Strategies aligned with student and educator learning goals				

(Continued)

Elements	Expert Use	Competent Use	Emerging Use	No Use
Application of the learning with local support at the work site • Ongoing support and assistance provided by coaches, team members, and external consultants • Adequate time frame so that high-fidelity or high-quality use of new strategies is achieved				
Use of evidence to monitor and refine implementation • Formative data are collected to confirm implementation • Data are used to refine and improve implementation rather than evaluate • Data are used to make midcourse corrections in professional learning when necessary • Explicit definitions of expected practice are developed • Colleagues may be involved in collecting classroom data				

Elements	Expert Use	Competent Use	Emerging Use	No Use
Evaluation of results • Uses SMART goals as the basis of results for both students and educators • Answers the question, "Have we accomplished our intended goals and are there other results that were not intentional?"				

Index

Measures of Academic Progress
(MAP), 63–64
Michigan, 6–7

National Merit, 62
National Writing Project (NWP):
author's chair strategy, 10
professional learning community,
9–10, 14
Newsweek, 62
No Child Left Behind Act (2000),
2–3, 62

Observations, 43, 51
Outcomes:
Learning Forward standards, x
professional learning communities,
2–3, 5, 7
school culture outcomes, 5
student achievement, 2–3, 5
teacher practice outcomes, 2–3, 5
Outside experts, 53

Partnerships, 51
Peer observations, 43, 51
Peers Supporting Peers, 23*f,* 24
Peres, Jason, 70–71, 74
Pilot learning team, 27, 33, 42
Pink, Daniel, 67
Poverty, 2
Principal role:
Blue Valley School District
(Kansas), 76
learning community development,
25–26, 27–28
Professional culture, 6–7, 12–13,
57–58
Professional learning communities:
accountability, 2–4
challenges of, 12–14
characteristics of, 1
collaboration, 13, 14–15
communities of practice, 4–5
contexts for, 6, 8–12
contribution-beyond-community
element, 11–12, 14, 15
current interest in, 2–4

current knowledge regarding, 4–8
data analysis, 7, 14
developmental conditions, 5–6
developmental stages, 7–8
educational policy initiatives,
2–4, 62
effectiveness studies, 5–6
equity, 2–3
implications of, 14–15
Leadership for Tomorrow's Schools
(LTS), 10–12, 14
leadership skills, 3, 7, 10–12
learning designs, 4
Learning Forward standards, ix
National Writing Project (NWP),
9–10, 14
outcomes, 2–3, 5, 7
professional culture, 6–7, 12–13,
57–58
pseudo-community, 8
purpose/vision commitment,
13, 15
reflective practice, 4–5
resources, 4–5, 14
school culture bureaucracy, 12–13,
57–58
school culture outcomes, 5
Southern Maine Partnership,
9, 10–12
strong-teacher communities, 7
strong-traditional teaching
communities, 7
structured work schedules, 5–6, 8
student achievement outcomes,
2–3, 5
teacher-centered reform, 3
teacher centers, 3
teacher-led reform, 3
teacher practice outcomes, 2–3, 5
teacher/student learning focus,
13–14, 15
time management, 13, 14–15
weak teaching communities, 6–7
Programme for International Student
Assessment (PISA), 61
Pseudo-community, 8
Purpose/vision commitment, 13, 15

CORWIN

A SAGE Company

The Corwin logo—a raven striding across an open book—represents the union of courage and learning. Corwin is committed to improving education for all learners by publishing books and other professional development resources for those serving the field of PreK–12 education. By providing practical, hands-on materials, Corwin continues to carry out the promise of its motto: **"Helping Educators Do Their Work Better."**

Advancing professional learning for student success

Learning Forward (formerly National Staff Development Council) is an international association of learning educators committed to one purpose in K–12 education: Every educator engages in effective professional learning every day so every student achieves.